Before Things Fall Apart:
Preparing to Care for Mom and Dad

Barbara McVicker

More Caregiving
Support and Information
From Barbara!

Before Things Fall Apart—The Workbook

Before Things Fall Apart: The Essential Workbook on Caring for Mom and Dad
Caregiving just got easier—with the Essential Workbook! This companion workbook to *Before Things Fall Apart* is designed just for caregivers. Loaded with helpful checklists, *The Essential Workbook* streamlines all your crucial caregiving tasks—assessments, appointments, downsizing, organizing important documents, and more. Get the most out of *Before Things Fall Apart* with this handy workbook.

Stuck in the Middle—The Book

Stuck in the Middle: Shared Stories and Tips on Caring for Mom and Dad
Over 75 million people are caregivers. These are their stories. Based on Barbara's interviews with healthcare professionals and caregivers, this book capture the realities, sorrows, and joys of caregiving. Useful tips included in every chapter provide helpful information as well.

Stuck in the Middle—The Television Special

Stuck in the Middle: Caring for Mom and Dad *AS SEEN ON PUBLIC TELEVISION*
Hosted by Barbara, this 90-minute DVD prepares adult caregivers to face the challenges of caring for their parents. Viewers learn how to assess their parents' needs, gather essential documents, communicate with their siblings, and build a successful caregiving team. This helpful, heartfelt special first appeared on public television.

Order today at: www.BarbaraMcVicker.com

Before Things Fall Apart:
Preparing to Care for Mom and Dad

Barbara McVicker

Stories by Jim Berg
Lyrics by Karen Taylor-Good

Edited by Katherine Matthews

ISBN: 978-0-9853896-2-8

Edited by: Katherine Matthews
Cover Design: Stewart A. Williams Design
Author Photo: Klatte Photography
Stories by: Jim Berg
Lyrics by: Karen Taylor-Good

Disclaimer

This book is intended to provide general information about caregiving for the elderly. The author
and publisher specifically disclaim all responsibility for any liability, loss, or risk, personal or
otherwise, which is incurred as a consequence, directly or indirectly, by the use and application
of any of the contents of this book. Please be aware that each of the 50 states in the United States
has different requirements for medical and financial documents. Medical information is
constantly changing and being updated. The content of this book is not meant to be a substitute
for professional advice. If expert assistance is required, the services of a competent professional
should be sought.

1. Aging Parents – Care   2. Caregivers   3. Family Relationships – Aging Parents

Ordering: www.BarbaraMcVicker.com

Other books by Barbara McVicker:
  Stuck in the Middle: Shared Stories and Tips on Caring for Mom and Dad
  Before Things Fall Apart: The Essential Workbook on Caring for Mom and Dad

Acknowledgements

There are many people whose efforts made this book possible. One deserves special recognition, my editor Katherine Matthews. She took my oral content, papers, and checklists, and fashioned a coherent compilation. Her organization and attention to detail captured the content and created a readable roadmap for the overwhelmed caregiver. She had assistance from Darby McVicker Puglielli, my daughter, a very positive force in *Stuck in the Middle: Shared Stories and Tips on Caring for Mom and Dad* and now in this new book. I also want to thank Constance Faddis, who polished the manuscript during the final phases.

I was privileged to have creative contributions by Jim Berg and Karen Taylor-Good. Several national experts added their tips and content. Thank you to Francine Russo, Meggin McIntosh, Marie Gibson, Julie Hall, Viki Kind, and Martin Sabel. You will be supported by their additional information. Attorney William J. Browning, CELA, assisted on the chapter about legal documents.

The cover design was created by Stewart Williams. The photo was shot by Klatte Photography.

Extraordinary help and support came from my wonderful family, Ryan, Darby, and Bob. My two children encouraged me to provide a lifeline to caregivers, and share my knowledge and emotional support. My husband, Bob, provided crucial, unending support as I worked nonstop on the books and the public television special, *Stuck in the Middle: Caring for Mom and Dad*.

Thanks to all of you!

Table of Contents

INTRODUCTION: Preparing to Care

Caregiving is a very important job. It's also a tough job with big challenges and wonderful rewards. By preparing yourself to care for Mom and Dad, you can reduce the stresses and demands of the caregiving experience on everyone—*especially you.*

Want to be a better, happier caregiver? This book is a great place to begin. My eight-step plan will help you start off on the right foot as you begin caregiving. Each chapter covers one step of the plan and focuses on providing essential information, useful strategies, and helpful advice for people just beginning the caregiving experience.

I'll give you an overview of each of the eight steps later in this Introduction, as well as several additional resources that you may find valuable immediately. I'll also invite you to visit my website for more helpful caregiver information. First, though, let me tell you my own caregiving story.

Barbara's Story

Whether you are already a caregiver for elderly parents, or just thinking ahead (good for you!) about your parents' future, I believe you will find my story helpful. I wish that I had been better prepared for caregiving. After you've read my story, you'll understand why it's so important to know what to expect, and how valuable it is to have experience-based information about ways to handle Mom and Dad's changing needs.

Everything under Control

One summer morning, I was sitting on my deck with a cup of coffee, listening to the breeze rustle through the trees. So peaceful. Tomorrow, my family would set off for a wonderful week at the lake. I was looking forward to relaxing with my husband and two kids.

I'm very organized, so I'd made all of the necessary arrangements to leave town on vacation. I had cleaned the house and done the laundry. I'd packed our suitcases and gassed up the car. Once I put the finishing touches on a grant proposal for work, I would be ready to go. Getting ready had taken a lot of preparation, but I knew that all my work would be worth it.

I was especially looking forward to spending time with my kids, who would be heading off to college in several years. Once they were gone, my husband and I would have plenty of time to relax and travel. I would finally have time for myself, too. The future looked wonderful. I had my whole life planned out!

Then the phone rang. My serenity evaporated. I didn't feel like answering it, but I stood up and headed inside. Sighing, I stepped into the kitchen and picked up the receiver.

The Crisis

The deep voice on the other end belonged to a police officer, calling from my parents' bank.

"Are you Herman's daughter?" the officer asked.

"Yes," I said.

"Your father's bank just notified us that he's been sending large sums of money to Canada over the last two weeks. Mrs. McVicker, are you aware of this?"

"No." I felt stunned, as if someone had slapped me in the face. "My dad? I don't understand."

The officer told me that, five days ago, my father had received a call from someone identifying himself as a representative of the Canadian Lottery. This person told my dad that he had won the "Mega Bucks" prize and could collect his million dollars after he paid $68,000 to the lottery officials to cover Canadian taxes. But he needed to send the money immediately or risk forfeiting his prize.

My Dad had stopped driving several years ago and rarely walked farther than to the end of the driveway to retrieve the newspaper. But after the "representative" called, Dad trudged ten blocks to the bank to get a cashier's check for thousands of dollars, which he sent to Canada. He made that trip three times!

My father had been scammed.

I was shocked. This made no sense. Dad had always held so tightly to his money. When I was a kid, he would refuse to buy ice cream cones for my sister and me. He'd tell us that we were selfish even to ask.

And now he had mailed $68,000 to a complete stranger. Something was terribly wrong.

Everything Changes

To prevent the scammers from stealing more money, I had to shut down all financial accounts associated with my parents' names, immediately. Instead of leaving on vacation, I spent the next 24 hours frantically closing their bank accounts, credit cards, stocks, Social Security, savings . . . everything.

Not wanting to disappoint my family, I agreed to a shortened vacation. I felt so tired, fragile, and overwhelmed that I sobbed softly for the whole eight-hour car trip to the lake. I felt stressed and confused and couldn't stop asking myself, "How did we get in such a mess?"

And I was angry. Incredibly angry!

I was angry at my parents! I had tried my best to keep them safe. I'd bought an answering machine for them. When I stopped by their house every day after work, I would listen to the messages and help them decide who to call back so they didn't get fooled by fake charities or shady sales offers. Using television shows, I educated them about scams against the elderly. I told them to not answer the door. Dad had been a businessman and Mom had been a teacher, so I knew they were smart, and I tried to be respectful of their independence. For years, they had taken care of our whole family, so I figured they could certainly watch out for themselves.

I never imagined that either of them would make such an ill-advised and *expensive* mistake.

But, as angry as I was at them, **I was absolutely furious with myself!** I felt embarrassed and humiliated. I kicked myself for not noticing the signs that my parents had changed. When my kids were little, my night table had been piled high with Dr. Spock and other books on raising kids, but I *never* thought about studying up on what to expect from Mom and Dad as they got older. I had been ready for my two-year-old's temper tantrums, but when my mother started digging in her heels and resisting the smallest change, I felt surprised and confused. I knew what kind of trouble 13-year-old boys could get into, but I never imagined that my own father would secretly send money to Canada.

I hadn't paid attention to the warning signs.

Mom had been a tidy housekeeper. Dad had kept their finances in perfect order. I didn't consider poking around my mom's refrigerator for spoiled food or examining my dad's checkbook. I shrugged off the piles of unopened mail on their desk. I didn't think about how my parents now slept until noon and were showering less often. Sometimes, when I came by after work, Mom and Dad would still be in their pajamas. When they stopped doing laundry, I picked up the piles of smelly clothes and washed them at my house.

I didn't want to intrude. I didn't want to have any uncomfortable conversations. I didn't question why they were doing things more slowly, or not at all. Every time a red flag popped up, I missed it or ignored it. As I looked back over the past few years, the path leading to this crisis became clear and I realized that my life had changed. Forever.

My parents needed my help. **Without me, things would fall apart.**

My life had taken a sudden, unexpected detour. That wonderful future I'd imagined while sitting on my deck vanished. My busy days as wife, mother, and employee were about to become infinitely more complicated. Somehow, my parents and I had traded roles, and I was supposed to take care of them now. Life was already hectic and demanding, and now I was stuck in the middle of three generations, with everyone depending on me.

And I was not ready. Not at all.

Most people are pushed into the role of caregiver by a crisis, just as I was. Maybe the hospital will phone you with the news that your mom has broken her hip and needs surgery. Or you'll find out that your dad hasn't paid the insurance bill for months and the policy was cancelled. You will probably step into the middle of a crisis to discover that your parents haven't prepared any financial or medical documents. You won't know whether they want to stay in their house or move to an assisted living community. You and your siblings won't have a plan for sharing the caregiving responsibilities fairly.

You will be overwhelmed, uninformed, and completely stressed out. Just as I was.

So, my question to you is . . . are you ready? **Are you ready?**

I want you to have the essential information and emotional support that you need *before* that inevitable phone call.

Stuck in the Middle

I cared for my parents for nearly as long as it took me to raise my children. My parents both died in their 90s, and I spent ten years helping them struggle through the final decade of their lives. I know the loneliness, guilt, anger, and sorrows of caregiving. I also know the joys, such as watching my mom develop a wonderful new friendship when she moved into an assisted living community.

Caregiving is a very tough job. When you have kids, everyone is willing to listen to your problems and offer advice. But no one wants to talk to a stressed-out caregiver about Mom's weak bladder or Dad's unprovoked rages. It's not cute when your mother accuses you of stealing her jewelry or your father drives his car into a ditch. All through my adult life, my friends have been invaluable sources of information and support. But when I looked around for a friendly mentor—someone who had already cared for aging parents—I realized that I was the first of my friends to face these challenges. So I looked other places for advice. But all I could find was a handful of books on caregiving, and very few websites. I blundered my way through those ten years of caregiving, never feeling like I got it right, always surprised by the next crisis, and usually overwhelmed.

I tell people that taking care of your parents, particularly when they are still living in their home, turns you into the CEO of a two-person nursing home. You must oversee everything—housekeeping, meals, laundry, medications, doctors, finances, legal issues, hiring (and firing) outside help, and a whole assortment of other challenges. I developed what I call "caregiver ADHD" as I made daily rounds between my office, my parents' home, my house, the soccer fields, the pharmacy, and the grocery store while squeezing in laundry and cooking and bill-paying for two households.

I felt **constantly stuck in the middle**—caring for my children and my parents while trying to manage a full-time job. *I was stuck* in the cardiologist's office with my mom when I needed to be picking up kids for the soccer carpool or sitting at my computer pounding out a grant proposal to meet a deadline. *I was stuck* because Mom and Dad refused to talk to me when I tried to map out a plan that honored their wishes for housing, finances, and medical treatment. *I was stuck* between wanting to help them and wanting to scream because of the constant conflicts.

One of my clearest memories? Changing Dad's diaper on a cold January afternoon, and then turning around to change my grandson's diaper.

Standing there, all I could think was, *I am stuck in the middle!*

Life after Caregiving

For ten years, I cared for my parents. I helped them stay in their home for as long as possible. After Mom and Dad moved to a continuing care retirement community, I cleaned out their house and sold it to provide them with enough funds to stay in their new home. I monitored my mother's diabetes and my father's dementia. I visited them every day. I ate hundreds of lunches with my mom and played many, many hands of UNO with her and her newfound friends. Dad passed away first; Mom died two years later, after shattering her hip.

After they both were gone, I felt completely drained. Physically, mentally, and emotionally. Worst of all, I was haunted by the picture of my wonderful kids struggling through the same heartbreaking experiences with me and their father, without support or cooperation or planning.

While I couldn't change what had happened to me, I *could* **change the future for my kids.** I desperately wanted to remember the lessons I had learned while caring for my parents, so I wrote down a list of 51 things that I was going to do differently. The title? "I'll Be Darned if I'm Going to Do This to My Kids." I pledged to live in a positive way "when it is my turn to be taken care of." I would try new things, keep my body moving, listen to suggestions from friends and family, move to appropriate housing, and stop driving "when my children ask me to." I wouldn't criticize, holds grudges, or say, "I wish I was dead."

Everyone heard about the list because I couldn't stop talking about it. Finally, I printed it out, got it notarized, and laminated it. I handed the plastic-coated paper to my two kids, who were now in their twenties, and said, "When I'm older, and the time comes that you need to talk to me about making changes and I start arguing, pull out this list. Wave it in my face. Tell me, 'Look at this. You said you were going to listen to us, Mom. You even had it *notarized*!'"

When I mentioned my list, people would tell me their own stories of caregiving. I soon realized how many adults out there needed comfort and advice about the caregiving experience. I decided to write a book, and began gathering stories from people who had faced the challenges of caring for their parents. Some stories were wonderful and uplifting while others were emotionally wrenching. After we spoke, these caregivers actually *thanked* me for listening to their tales, because no one else had ever done that. I also had discussions with healthcare experts and interviewed eldercare professionals. **I assembled the stories, along with helpful information for caregivers, into a book (my first) called** *Stuck in the Middle: Shared Stories and Tips on Caring for Mom and Dad.*

I became a speaker, talking to audiences about caregiving for their parents and about planning ahead instead of waiting for a crisis. Within a few years, I was working with healthcare professionals, caregivers, financial institutions, human resource departments, and sales personnel. I was featured in *The Wall Street Journal, AARP,* and *USA Today*, and appeared on CNN, NPR, and NBC. I also hosted and co-produced the public television special *Stuck in the Middle: Caring for Mom and Dad.*

When I speak, I talk to caregivers about the huge physical, financial, and emotional challenges of their new responsibilities. Many find themselves torn between financing their aging parents' needs, their kids' college tuition fund, and their own retirement savings. The conflicts, role reversals, and constant demands of caregiving make them feel anxious, stressed, and weary. Most caregivers struggle to keep themselves healthy enough, both emotionally and physically, to hold up under the strain of so many demands.

After talking to hundreds of people, I realized that **caregivers need much more information and support than I could give them in a single speech.** So I decided to write a second book, one that would include everything I wish I had known at the moment when I got that awful phone call from the police about my father.

Before Things Fall Apart: The Book and the Workbook

I designed *Before Things Fall Apart: Preparing to Care for Mom and Dad* as a lifeline for you and your fellow caregivers. This book is a quick-start guide to caring for your aging parents. It combines essential information and emotional support into one concise, easy-to-use book.

The eight chapters that follow will walk you through the eight essential steps you need to do to prepare to caregive.

Use this book *now* to prepare to care for your parents, even if they are still in good physical and mental health. *Now* is the best time to plan for the coming years. By being proactive, you will create a happier, healthier future for your whole family.

If you are starting in a crisis situation, you can use *Before Things Fall Apart* to educate yourself quickly about caregiving and move forward in a sensible, orderly way.

To help you stay organized during caregiving, I've also compiled a companion workbook—*Before Things Fall Apart: The Essential Workbook on Caring for Mom and Dad*. Loaded with useful checklists and helpful tips, this workbook follows the same eight-step plan as *Before Things Fall Apart*.

Best of all, once you've started caregiving for Mom and Dad, these books can also help you and your own children work together to design a shared plan for your *own* future. Take control now and plan ahead. It may be the most valuable gift that you'll ever give to your family.

--Barbara

The Eight Steps to Preparing to Care for Mom and Dad

Through my work with caregivers across the country, I've discovered that adult children

caring for their parents need two things: **essential information** and **emotional support**. *Before*

Things Fall Apart provides both.

Using this book as a guide, you can take one, sane, manageable step at a time to prepare for

the caregiving experience. If you're *already* caring for Mom and Dad, you'll find strategies, tips,

and advice here to make your life easier. My goal is give you a quick understanding of the basics

of caregiving, and help you to move forward in the most efficient way possible.

Here is a quick overview of the **eight steps.** Follow this plan to **make caregiving easier,**

less stressful, and more effective:

1. **Educate yourself about the caregiving experience.** This is a new stage in your life and your parents' lives. You can prepare for the upcoming challenges by learning more about caregiving. Knowing more means fewer surprises, more successes, and better control of what may often seem uncontrollable. See *Chapter 1: Are You Ready?*

2. **Assess Mom and Dad's situation.** Get a realistic picture of how well your parents are functioning right now. Carrying out an assessment will reveal the challenges facing Mom and Dad. It will provide the tools you need to help solve problems, improve daily life, and ensure safety. Assessments give you helpful information that you can share with siblings and your parents' doctors, as well. See *Chapter 2: Stop, Look, and Listen.*

3. **Learn how to talk to Mom and Dad.** Knowing your parents' wishes is a crucial part of caregiving. Many of us don't know how to talk to our parents about serious issues, so we keep putting off those important conversations. This chapter will help you get talking. See *Chapter 3: I Love You and I Want to Help You.*

4. **Learn how to have productive family meetings.** Good communication within families is crucial to successful caregiving. Learn how to hold family meetings that enable you, your siblings, and other appropriate relatives to create a caregiving plan and prioritize what needs to be done, and when, and by whom. See *Chapter 4: We're All in This Together.*

5. **Organize important documents.** There are five essential medical and financial documents that your parents need to have in place as they get older. Help them gather or create these documents now to reduce anxiety and prevent big problems in the future. *See Chapter 5: Don't Wait!*

6. **Get ready to deal with doctors and hospitals.** Your parents will need your help with medical issues. Learn great tips for organizing your parents' medical information, accompanying them to doctor appointments, getting the most out of the visits, and helping your parents when they are in the hospital. See *Chapter 6: Please Sit Down and Fill Out This Form.*

7. **Declutter Mom and Dad's home.** Having a tidier home helps your parents function better and stay healthier. An uncluttered house is also easier to pack and move when the time comes for your parents to leave their current home. See *Chapter 7: Too Much Stuff!*

8. **Research housing options.** Educate yourself now about housing options for seniors, since there's a very good chance that your parents will depend on in-home care or need to move into a more supportive environment in the future. See *Chapter 8: Time for a Change.*

Still feeling like caregiving is too big a job for you right now? That's okay—I understand.

Lots of caregivers feel that way at first. **Just take it one step at a time and** *you will get it done.*

And I'll be here to help you. **You are not alone**. If you've got a question to ask, a story to tell, or just need a shoulder to cry on, send me a note at: *www.BarbaraMcVicker.com*

I can't wait to hear from you.

Some of us receive applause quite often
Others simply roll around in wealth
But if this life were fair, there is a group out there
Who'd be richest and most famous as well

    Caretakers of our bodies, midwives of our souls
    Never underestimate the lofty place you hold
    You make such a difference, you change people's lives
    You are angels.........in disguise

Don't worry, I won't give away your cover
I can just pretend that I don't know
But when we are in need, it's really plain to see
You were sent to help us here below

    Caretakers of our bodies, midwives of our souls
    Never underestimate the lofty place you hold
    Patient, understanding, strong and kind and wise
    You are angels.........in disguise

And when you do your magic, it's such important work
Bringing some of heaven's love back down to earth

    Caretakers of our bodies, midwives of our souls
    Never underestimate the lofty place you hold
    Your hands are God's hands, His light shines through your eyes
    You are angels, you are angels
    You are angels.........in disguise

"Angels in Disguise"
By: Karen Taylor Good, Ed Tossing, & Lisa Aschmann

Are You Ready?—
Learn the Basics of Caregiving

- **Identify the 5 phases of caregiving**
- **Prepare for the 5 challenges of caregiving**
- **Address the 5 most common conflicts during caregiving**
- **Learn about the 5 benefits of caregiving**
- **Practice the 5 cures of caregiving**

You might be a caregiver if . . .

- You contemplate "accidently" dropping your cell phone into the toilet so that you can have some time to yourself.

- You ask why the mailbox at the end of the driveway is knocked over and your Dad mutters, "the wind."

- The highlight of your week was winning the bingo game at Mom's assisted living facility.

- Mom and Dad's pharmacist sees you so often that she friended you on Facebook.

- Your list for a late-night run to the drugstore includes Excedrin for you, Midol for your daughter, and Depends for your mother.

- You've been in a doctor's office eight times in the past two months, but you haven't seen your own physician in two years.

- You feel like the CEO of a two-person nursing home.

Caregiving for your parents is one of the most important jobs you will ever have. It's also complicated, exhausting, fulfilling, and—at times—overwhelming. No one tells you this. My life changed abruptly with a phone call telling me my father had been scammed out of $68,000. I remember feeling confused, angry, sad, and overwhelmed.

I already had two children, a husband, and a house to care for. How could I possibly manage my parents' lives, too? I had a career that demanded time and attention. How could I continue to do a good job at work? My parents didn't get along with each other, and always resisted new ideas. How would I convince them to drastically change their lives? I had so many questions, and very few answers.

As I started the job of caregiving for my parents, I wish I had known how long the journey would take, how challenging the experience would be, and how to triumph over the conflicts ahead.

When you receive that inevitable phone call telling you that Mom or Dad needs your help, will you be prepared? I wasn't. What about you . . . Are you ready? Are you organized and knowledgeable and prepared for caregiving?

If not, read on.

Caregiving: THE 5 PHASES

The caregiving experience encompasses five phases: Caregiving 101, Caregiving 911, Continuous Support, Saying Goodbye, and Mourning. In many cases, the caregiving experience will cover a long stretch of time—from five to ten years. The length of each phase depends on the state of your parents' physical and cognitive health.

Phase 1: *Caregiving 101*

Caregiving 101 begins when changes in your parents' physical or cognitive abilities become apparent. Most of the time, these changes creep in quietly. By paying attention to shifts in Mom's and Dad's behaviors, you can help prevent future crises. Classic warning signs include:

- Neglect of household chores like vacuuming, dusting, and laundry
- Unpaid bills and/or a checkbook that hasn't been balanced for several months
- Unexplained dents in your parents' car
- A significant change in sleep habits, such as not getting up until noon
- Erratic or unhealthy meals

None of these changes is life-threatening, so the tendency is to ignore them and tell yourself, "That's just the way Mom and Dad are now. It's no big deal." In this situation, denial and avoidance are natural reactions. You don't want to appear nosy or bossy. You don't want to parent your parents. It's hard to admit that Mom and Dad aren't the same independent and capable people that they once were. I understand this—I acted exactly the same way, so I am speaking from experience when I tell you: *Now is the ideal time to prepare for the future—for both you and your parents.*

Acting now will make a ***huge*** difference when a crisis hits. The perfect time to start preparing for the future is when your parents turn 70. If you've missed that deadline, don't worry—you have even more incentive to get to work now! Several of these tasks, especially those involving legal issues, must be completed while your parents are mentally capable, so acting now is essential.

The first phase of caregiving is the optimal time to—

- Complete essential documents—wills, trusts, and powers of attorney
- Gather medical histories
- Become familiar with your parents' medical facilities and doctors
- Discuss hiring outside help to make life easier and safer for Mom and Dad
- Declutter their house
- Begin renovations that will improve safety and accessibility in their home
- Assist Mom and Dad with creating a housing plan for the future

- Agree on safe and practical parameters for driving
- Make decisions about the end-of-life phase

Completing this list involves work, but the results are worth the effort. You and your parents will feel secure and in control. You will know that everyone is prepared for a crisis. Making decisions during a crisis is *always* more difficult, time-consuming, and stressful. Avoid it if you can. This brings us to. . . .

Phase 2: *Caregiving 911*

A crisis strikes. There are many different scenarios—a car accident, hospitalization, loss of mobility, financial troubles—but the result is the same. Your parent desperately needs your help. You have to begin caregiving immediately but you are unprepared, fearful, and overwhelmed. You are deeply worried about your parent, and you're being asked to make a hundred decisions without enough information or much knowledge of your parent's wishes.

This is the most common way that people begin the caregiving process. Caregiving 911 often requires an adult child to drop everything in order to address the urgent needs of a parent. After my father secretly sent that $68,000 to scam artists because they told him that he had won the Canadian lottery, I spent days closing accounts and reviewing my parents' finances as fast as I could. I had to ignore my husband and kids, postpone our family vacation, and take time off from my job. My future, which I thought I had all planned out, was suddenly a big question mark. Adding to the anxiety and uncertainty was the fact that I had no idea what the future held for my mother and father.

Beginning your caregiving experience during a crisis can be frightening and overwhelming. But I have some good news. You will get through this phase. I've designed each chapter in this book to help you quickly understand and address the most crucial aspects of caregiving.

If you've planned ahead with your parents and gone through Caregiving 101 *before* a crisis occurs, this phase will be *much easier*. Since you already have Mom's and Dad's medical and financial documents in order, and have discussed with them what to do in an emergency, you know what to do. You are ready to handle the challenges presented by any sudden disaster.

Phase 3: *Continuous Support*

No one tells you about this phase, but here is where the true day-to-day caregiving happens. Often lasting for five to ten years or longer, Phase 3 involves watching over Mom and Dad as they age, monitoring their physical health, tracking their mental capabilities, and helping them make decisions—or, at times, making the decisions yourself. As each year passes, you should expect that your parents will face new challenges and be able to do less for themselves.

This phase of Continuous Support encompasses the most time-consuming and demanding caregiving tasks. Initially, you may take Mom and Dad to the doctor and help them with housework, laundry, and cooking. As this phase progresses, the jobs get tougher and more time-intensive as your parents need more help with the acts of daily living (ADLs). Many caregivers will enlist outside help, such as housekeepers, in-home healthcare aides, or nurses to enable their parents to remain in the home. This is called "aging in place," and often involves remodeling Mom and Dad's residence to improve safety and accessibility.

Phase 3 also covers the move from home to a facility where parents can benefit from more supervision, access to daily medical care, and safer surroundings. Although the day-to-day physical burdens are usually relieved by this move, caregivers still have many responsibilities to handle.

Phase 4: *Saying Goodbye*

This is the end-of-life period. During this phase, your elderly parent is actively dying. This phase can be a gift or a burden, depending upon the amount of preparation you and your family have done around end-of-life and funeral issues. I encourage you and your siblings to have open discussions about the dispersion of assets before your parents reach this phase. You will each be struggling with emotional and mental turmoil as you say goodbye to your parent. Expecting anyone to make calm, rational decisions while a parent is dying is unreasonable. Be kind to yourselves, and have these discussions early in the process.

Hospice can be an invaluable resource at this time. Hospice provides comforting end-of-life care, either in a facility or in the home, and can be tremendously helpful with finding resources and providing emotional support for the entire family. Working through those tough end-of-life decisions may be easier with Hospice support.

Phase 5: *Mourning*

After your parents pass away, life changes abruptly. For years, caregiving has consumed your time and energy. Your weekly schedule revolved around doctor appointments, visits to the assisted-care facility, and taking your parents out to lunch. Being a caregiver has been an essential part of your identity for a long time. Now that your parents are gone, who are you? How do you redefine yourself? What do you want to do now?

In addition to experiencing a loss of identity, you are grieving. Many experts estimate that this phase lasts three years. I think that everyone experiences grief differently, though, and this time will last as long as it lasts, and there's nothing wrong with that. People make their way through the classic five stages of grief—denial, anger, bargaining, depression, and acceptance—in their own ways. Grief doesn't follow a straight line through this process, but can skip from stage to stage or get stuck in one place until the mourner is ready to move on. This is a natural process and can be instructive, healing, and even transformational. Grief counseling can be invaluable at this point, especially for caregivers who feel lost or depressed.

I have a business acquaintance, Jeanne Safer, PhD, who wrote a book called *Death Benefits*. At first, I assumed the book talked about dry issues such as life insurance and other death benefit packages. After looking through the book, I realized that *Death Benefits* details how loss of a parent can improve an adult child's life. Safer explains how adult children can redefine themselves after their parents' deaths. This last phase of caregiving can be a time of self-actualization, freedom, and increased energy, as well as deep sadness.

Caregiving: THE 5 CHALLENGES

Caregiving can be a tough business. When you know more about the challenges of caregiving, you are better prepared to deal with the effects.

Challenge 1: *Dealing with Powerful Emotions*

The emotions involved in caregiving are very powerful. Our relationships with our parents are emotionally rich, complex, and deeply felt. As a caregiver, you may be feeling:

- **Sadness.** You see your parents losing their independence. You see them struggling with physical and cognitive impairment. You see how their quality of life has diminished and you miss the people they used to be.

- **Anger.** You feel angry because you were looking forward to having time (finally) for yourself because the kids were older, but now you spend all your free time taking care of Mom and Dad. You may also feel angry because you are not being thanked for your hard work, or because your siblings are not sharing fairly with caregiving.

- **Denial.** You can't really believe that Mom and Dad are no longer able to care properly for themselves. It feels unnatural and disrespectful to be parenting your parents. No one else in the family wants to talk about it, so you don't feel comfortable bringing it up.

- **Guilt.** You feel *guilty*. My audiences tell me that guilt is the *number one* emotion that they experience. They feel guilty about everything, including not spending enough time with their parents or their own families, not giving their jobs enough attention, wanting some time for themselves, and seeing their parents unhappy but not being able to change the situation.

- **Stress.** You feel *overwhelmed*. You can't find enough hours in the day to accomplish everything. You are torn between kids, career, and your parents. Your marriage is suffering because you don't have enough time and energy for your spouse. You are stressed out physically with fatigue, headaches, and other physical symptoms. You are stressed out emotionally because you can't take care of everything. You are stressed financially because caregiving is consuming your time and money. For example, you may have cut back to part-time work in order to care for Mom and Dad, resulting in a loss of income and benefits or you may be supporting your parents financially.

You feel like you're drowning, but you don't have anyone to talk to about the challenges of caregiving. Chatting about diapering Dad is not nearly as socially acceptable as talking about diapering your kids or your grandkids.

Challenge 2: *Facing the Losses*

As your parents age, they experience loss in nearly every aspect of their lives. When you step into the role of caregiver, you also struggle with loss.

Your losses due to caregiving may include:

- Your free time
- The ability to work without distraction or interruption
- Time with your own family
- Your money
- Your energy and health

Your parents are also experiencing loss because:

- Their health is deteriorating and, in most cases, will not improve
- Their eyesight, hearing, or mobility is now impaired
- Their treasured and trusted friends have passed away
- They are losing their independence, no matter how hard they work to prevent it
- They can no longer care for their home
- They may no longer be able to drive
- They may need to move from a house filled with memories

Challenge 3: *Starting in Crisis*

My life changed when I got a phone call from my father's bank telling me he'd been scammed. Your life may change when you get a call informing you that Mom is in the emergency room. Or that Dad lost control of his car and skidded through an intersection. Or that your parents' house is suddenly in foreclosure because they forgot to make the mortgage payments.

Caregiving often starts in a crisis, which adds to the stress and frustration. It's almost like being put down in the middle of a tornado and being told, "Figure it out!"

Challenge 4: *Being Unprepared*

I had educated myself about raising children and how to do my job. But I had *never* considered educating myself about caring for my aging parents. I didn't even want to think about caregiving for Mom and Dad. Then, when I suddenly ended up in the middle of that tornado, I had no idea what to do. Even after dealing with the initial crisis, I didn't sit down and look ahead to the future. Having a conversation with my parents about what to do when they got sick or needed to move out of the house was going to be difficult and stressful, so I avoided it. I simply moved from one problem to the next, putting out one fire after another. As a result, I was exhausted, angry, and anxious.

Don't fall into this trap. Plan ahead and design a long-term strategy for caregiving.

Challenge 5: *Meeting the Demands*

Caregiving is a marathon, not a sprint. Caregivers often devote up to 20 hours a week to help a sick or aging family member, and the average caregiving period lasts for years. This is a huge commitment of time, energy, and love. In a 2010 study, AARP estimates that all this unpaid care is worth about $450 billion a year nationally.

Not surprisingly, caregivers feel the effects of all these demands, especially if they are employed. Personal relationships often suffer. In fact, in Caring.com's 2009 study of Baby Boomers, over 80 percent of caregivers report that their efforts to help loved ones have placed stress on their marriages.

A Gallup Poll in 2010 revealed that full-time workers who are also **caregivers are significantly more likely than non-caregivers to experience health issues** such as depression, diabetes, hypertension, and pulmonary disease. In fact, the primary caregiver is often called the "hidden patient." Despite being preoccupied with their parents' healthcare, caregivers often take poor care of themselves. In a 2006 study conducted by Evercare and the National Alliance for Caregiving, over 50 percent of caregivers admitted that they skip their own doctor appointments. The same study also found that caregivers eat more poorly and exercise less than non-caregivers. The most sobering statistic? In 2007, The Ohio State University and the National Institute on Aging announced that caregiving has been shown to decrease your lifespan by up to *three years*.

Aside from the physical demands, **caregiving requires a lot of mental effort**, such as keeping track of Mom's and Dad's appointments, finances, prescriptions, health issues, and more. I have a friend who was caregiving for her parents while running her own business and participating actively at her church. My friend was always proactive about her health, so when she started having trouble with her memory and concentration, she made an appointment at a comprehensive gerontology clinic.

My friend underwent tests that included memorizing a long list of words, summarizing a story, and playing a word association game. There were also the usual blood tests, family history questionnaires, and a physical check-up. After the tests, the gerontologist calmly explained that his diagnosis was mild cognitive impairment, which is sometimes a precursor to dementia. Stunned, she decided to get another opinion.

After talking to her and analyzing her test results, the second doctor had a completely different diagnosis. He assured my friend that she was not developing dementia, but actually suffered from "cognitive distraction" due to her over-the-top busy life. He told her to declutter her office, check her e-mail only twice daily, and take an hour off each day to just sit quietly. Most importantly, she was to set boundaries with her aging parents. She didn't need to be at their beck-and-call 24 hours a day, seven days a week. After following the doctor's suggestions for six months, my friend regained her impressive memory and organizational skills, and felt better physically and emotionally.

Caregiving can be financially demanding as well. Caregivers often spend their own money to help support Mom and Dad. In addition, some people quit their jobs or decide to work only part-time once they realize how much time caregiving requires. If you are considering changing your employment situation, be sure to consider *all* the repercussions. Your losses may be far more costly than you realize. The 2011 *MetLife Study of Caregiving Costs to Working Caregivers: Double Jeopardy for Baby Boomers Caring for Their Parents* found that caregivers who are over 50 years old and leave their jobs lose hundreds of thousands of dollars in pensions, healthcare benefits, Social Security benefits, and wages. Based on the MetLife statistics, actual losses for the average caregiver come to over $300,000.

What can you learn from these studies, stories, and statistics? **When you are taking care of Mom and Dad, it is crucial that you take care of yourself**. When warning my audiences about the demands of caregiving, I recite the instructions given by airline attendants at the beginning of the flight: "Always put on your own oxygen mask first, and then assist your child or companion." If you take care of yourself, you will be able to help your loved ones . . . but if you expend all your energy taking care of other people, then you risk giving so much of yourself away that you eventually will have nothing left to offer. You won't be able to help anyone, including yourself.

Caregiving: THE 5 MOST COMMON CONFLICTS

When it comes to caregiving, I can guarantee you one thing—you will have conflicts with your parents. Even if you have a great relationship with Mom and Dad, caregiving forces you to deal with issues that will provoke anger, disagreement, disappointment, and compromise—on both sides. Which issues cause the most conflicts? **Housing, money, driving, making decisions about medical and financial documents, and coping with challenges of everyday life.** You can't avoid these topics, and the problems they pose are rarely simple or easy to solve. Conflicts arise because you and your parents have different priorities and beliefs concerning these five issues.

The shifting relationship with your parents makes dealing with conflicts even more challenging. For approximately 40 years, you have been the child and they have been the parents. Now the roles are reversed. You are caring for them. Although you don't want to tell them what to do or deprive them of their independence, you will probably need to take charge at some point in the caregiving process. Be aware that your parents are struggling with similar contradictions. While they want to maintain their self-sufficiency, Mom and Dad probably realize that they will need to depend on you for help, guidance, or protection in the future.

At times, dealing with these issues also involves your siblings or other relatives, and this can add to the turmoil. Even healthy families can become dysfunctional during caregiving. A crisis with your parents can dredge up sibling issues that date back to childhood: rivalries over who is the favorite child, arguments over who has the authority to make decisions, hurt feelings over past wrongs, and divided loyalties between brothers and sisters.

There are three ways to prepare for **dealing with conflicts involving your parents and siblings**:

1. **Try to avoid getting stuck in unhelpful patterns of conversation and behavior.** There are effective strategies you can use to talk with your family members. I recommend reading **Chapters 3 and 4** before you talk to your parents or siblings. These chapters are devoted to helping you and your family members get the most out of your conversations—while creating the least amount of discord.

2. **Attempt to understand the situation from your parents' point of view.** This doesn't necessarily mean that you agree with their viewpoint. They may be emotionally or cognitively unable to see the issue in a rational way. So, you can choose to be frustrated and angry about this or you can choose to understand your parents' concerns and help them deal with the situation in a constructive way.

3. **Educate yourself about the options and solutions available to your parents.** When your parents need help, simply pointing out the problem won't be enough. You must be able to offer a choice of solutions.

Most of the time, your parents' concerns don't spring simply from stubbornness or selfishness—although it may feel that way to you. When my father would get argumentative, demanding, or mean, I would take a deep breath and tell him firmly, "I love you but I'm not going to stand here and take this. I will come back tomorrow." Then I would leave. Although I felt a strong temptation to argue or act hurt, I realized that those actions would only worsen the situation and chip away at my self-respect. When I turned around and left the room, I wasn't abandoning my father . . . I was standing up for myself. I always told Dad that I would return, and I always did.

Don't be surprised if your parents act fearful or anxious when dealing with important issues. Remember that they will feel worse if you become angry or resentful. Stay calm. It's not about you.

Conflict 1: *Housing*

Your parents' current housing may not be well-suited to their changing needs, but convincing them to move can be a tremendous challenge. In a 2009 MetLife survey, only *one-third* of the respondents believed that they would need long-term care. Yet, according to statistics provided by AARP.com, over *two-thirds* of Americans who turned 65 in 2007 will need long-term care at some point. So, even if you and your parents don't believe it, there's a very good chance **that Mom and Dad will need to move out of their home** and into housing designed for seniors at some point during the caregiving process.

Your Concerns	*Your Parents' Concerns*
You worry about their health and safety.	They don't want you to tell them how to live their lives.
You don't think they are getting enough exercise or stimulation living by themselves.	They want to remain independent.
You are physically, emotionally, or financially unable to do all the caregiving for your parents.	They don't want to be a burden, but they don't want to leave their house and move somewhere new and unknown either.

Conflict 2: *Money*

Seventy percent of adult children have never talked about money with their parents, according to a 2007 study by the National Alliance for Caregiving. Yet, caregivers often deplete their own savings to help their parents. The same study found that the average caregiver spends about $5500 a year supporting Mom and Dad.

Dealing with money issues is crucial, especially for your parents. Your entire family needs to know whether there is enough money to take care of Mom and Dad properly. Otherwise, you can't plan for the future—you won't know whether you should be planning to work past your retirement age to support them . . . or if they have enough money tucked away under their mattress to move into a great independent living apartment and take a cruise once a year.

Your Concerns	*Your Parents' Concerns*
Your parents' financial situation is unknown.	They believe money is a private matter and don't want to share their information.
You don't know if you need to help support them using your own funds.	They don't want to take your charity . . . *or* they assume that you will support them when they run out of money.
You worry that the bills aren't being paid on time, or that someone may be scamming your parents.	They want to take care of their own business affairs, even though they are struggling with memory or cognitive issues.

Conflict 3: *Driving*

Most caregivers are surprised to learn that **driving causes the biggest conflicts between caregivers and their parents**. This issue is so polarizing that bringing in a third party to mediate this conflict is often incredibly helpful. The third party can be a trusted friend, doctor, lawyer, the DMV, their insurance agent, or another professional who your parents hold in esteem.

Your Concerns	*Your Parents' Concerns*
You want your parents and other drivers to be safe.	They feel that being able to drive is convenient and allows them to be independent.
You don't have a clear idea of your parents' current driving abilities—*or* you know that their skills and response time are getting worse, but don't know what to do about it.	They each have over 50 years of experience and know how to drive well. In fact, they taught *you* how to drive.
You know of other, safer options, but these may be less convenient for your parents.	They don't want to depend on others for transportation or they are unaware of other options.

Conflict 4: *Medical and Financial Documents*

There are five essential documents that your parents need to have right now. These include a Last Will and Testament, a living will, a healthcare power of attorney, a financial power of attorney, and HIPAA forms that allow you access to their medical information. Many parents may also want to establish trusts and create a Do-Not-Resuscitate Order. All of these documents need to contain up-to-date information, be properly signed, and be executed in the state where your parents reside. Revisit these important documents every two to five years, or as their life circumstances change.

Your Concerns	*Your Parents' Concerns*
You don't know if your parents have a will.	They don't want to spend money and time on a will, or feel that creating one is too upsetting.
You are not listed on their HIPAA forms, so the doctor cannot share your parents' medical information with you.	They feel that their medical information is private.
You don't know if your parents have established any trusts.	They don't want to share their financial information.
Your parents haven't made any end-of-life decisions.	They think talking about death is morbid and upsetting.
Your parents haven't designated a healthcare power of attorney.	They want to believe that they can continue to take care of themselves health-wise.
Your parents haven't chosen a person to give financial power of attorney.	They don't want to give up control over their money.

Conflict 5: *Everyday Life*

As parents age, normal everyday activities often turn challenging or burdensome. Chores ranging from cooking dinner to mowing the lawn become more difficult. Routine tasks that are mentally demanding, such as paying bills, taking medications, and keeping doctor appointments, require more concentration and planning. Some of the most basic acts of daily living, such as showering and using the toilet, turn into struggles.

Your Concerns	*Your Parents' Concerns*
You want to make the house safer and more accessible.	They don't want their children telling them what to do in their own home.
You know they need help around the house.	They expect you to help them with the chores, because they don't want strangers in their home.
You worry that they can't maintain a healthy level of personal hygiene and grooming.	They see having a stranger help with bathing and grooming as embarrassing and an invasion of privacy.

Caregiving: THE 5 BENEFITS

Certain words come up again and again when we talk about caregiving: sadness, anger, denial, guilt, stress . . . sometimes it seems as though caregiving is nothing but hardship and negative emotions.

What about the good stuff?

The benefits of caregiving don't shout as loudly as the challenges, but **the positives are still there,** hidden under the day-to-day struggles. Some of the rewards of caregiving may not be evident until several years *after* your parents have passed away and you have had an opportunity to process their deaths and your caregiving experience. The subtle nature of these rewards doesn't diminish their significance or the positive influence that caregiving can have on your life and your family's lives.

Benefit 1: *Getting Closer*

Caregiving helps you form a deeper relationship with your parents. Just as they bonded with you by caring for your needs when you were younger, you can bond with them as you help them through this phase of their life. You and your parents are in this together and you need each other.

Benefit 2: *Doing the Right Thing*

Caregiving is an opportunity to repay your parents for the time, love, and support they have given you over the course of your lifetime. There can be deep satisfaction in seeing your life come full circle as you lovingly care for the same people who spent years raising you and supporting you in so many ways.

For those of us who have difficult parents, this reward can be harder to find. If your parents were selfish when they should have been giving, harsh when they should have been gentle, or cold when they should have been warm and loving, you may have trouble rising above your anger and pain in order to take care of them now.

As a caregiver, you may not get much appreciation from your parents and other family members. Sometimes, there just aren't any Hallmark moments between parents and children. So

I have three things to say to you that you may not be hearing from your family: "YOU are a wonderful daughter or son. You are a resilient person who is doing a very important job. Thank you so much."

Benefit 3: *Being a Role Model*

By your words and actions, you are showing other people how to be a good caregiver. Your children, your siblings, and your friends will be learning about caregiving by watching how you handle this situation. You are a great role model for your kids, showing them how and why we caregive for others. This impacts your children's current and future relationships with their friends, children, significant others, and you—especially when *you* become an elderly parent. This doesn't mean that you need to be perfect. Sometimes seeing how someone fails or puzzles their way through a problem is even more instructive than watching them succeed.

Benefit 4: *Saying "Good-bye"*

The caregiving period gives you the opportunity to say "good-bye" to your parents and prepare yourself for their eventual passing. You may want to use this time to say "I'm sorry" or "I forgive you." Caregiving provides many opportunities to show your parents how you feel about them, and to do those special activities that you may have been putting off. For you, saying "good-bye" might mean something as big as taking Dad on a trip to Italy, or something as small as snuggling with Mom while you both watch her favorite Cary Grant movies.

This time also presents a final chance to preserve your family's history and find out the answers to important questions. Ask your parents about their childhood, their own parents, their hometown, and their courtship, and then preserve these stories by writing them down or recording them. Share these with the entire family.

Benefit 5: *Dealing with Your Emotions*

Caregiving gives you an opportunity to face your emotions and process them. When I started caregiving for my parents, I felt like I was drowning in emotions. Going through the caregiving process gave me perspective and helped me see my parents in a new way.

17

I had to deal with difficult emotions from the very beginning. Shortly after I learned that Dad lost all that money to scammers, I drove to visit my sister. I was choked up with anger and sadness. I was still furious at my father. At the same time, I felt very anxious about caregiving for my parents.

As I talked to my sister, we recalled all the times we'd been dismissed, belittled, and judged by our parents. We grew more and more angry and frustrated. Together, we decided to try to rid ourselves of all this old history so we could get on with our own adult lives unencumbered.

My sister was renovating her home and a huge dumpster sat in the driveway to collect the construction debris. She also had a recycling bin full of glass bottles in the garage. We dragged ladders out to the driveway and started heaving bottles into the dumpster and naming each time our parents had hurt us.

This was for the time you showed up at my piano recital drunk. **Crash!** *This was for when you dismissed all my hard work in Advanced Physics class because I got a B+ instead of an A.* **Crash!** *This was for the never-ending stress at our house because you two argued constantly.* **Crash! Crash! Crash!**

Eventually, there were no more bottles left to fling. Sweating and sobbing, I hugged my sister. Then I realized that we also needed to remember the good times.

We collected a basket of rose petals from her garden and took two kayaks out onto the lake near her house. As we recalled each fond memory, my sister and I gently placed petals on the water, leaving a trail of pink behind us in the glistening lake. Crying, we forgave our parents and ourselves. Our emotions spent, my sister and I quietly paddled back to shore, and then watched from the dock as the breeze spread the rose petals across the water.

I felt exhausted and cleansed. For the first time in many years, I could think about my parents without resentment or anger. Now my sister and I could close the door on the past and move forward with a very different perspective. Instead of judging Mom and Dad solely on their actions, my sister and I now understood their intentions. We realized that they had done the best that they could, given their own circumstances.

If I had kept my feelings "bottled up" inside, or turned my anger on my parents, I would have hurt both them and myself. Find your own way of releasing the emotions that build up during caregiving. The power of your feelings during this time may surprise you. I would *never* have envisioned myself smashing bottles and shouting out my most painful memories, but I am so glad that I did. Letting go of those emotions let me move forward with a clearer mind and stronger heart, and helped me face the challenges of caregiving for my mother and father.

Caregiving: THE 5 CURES

Caregiving for your parents is one of the most demanding jobs that you will ever have. These five cures will help make that job easier, better, and more rewarding.

Cure 1: *Set Boundaries and Prioritize*

You can't do everything by yourself and you shouldn't try. Prioritize your caregiving tasks so that the most important jobs get the most attention and don't fret over the small stuff. Carefully consider what you can reasonably do and what you can't do . . . and then stick to it!

Cure 2: *Take Personal Time*

This is probably the most important cure . . . and the hardest to accomplish. Set aside time to read, socialize, take a long hot bath, or hang out at a coffeehouse. It's all right to put your parents out of your mind for a while. You need time to recharge your batteries and be free of the constant demands of caregiving.

Cure 3: *Do Research and Utilize Resources*

The more you know, the more you can accomplish as a caregiver. Information is power, and understanding the details of caregiving puts you in control. Reading this book is one way that you are taking positive steps towards becoming a better, more informed caregiver. There are also plenty of great resources available. I've listed some of my favorites at the end of this book.

Cure 4: *Join a Support Group and/or Find a Mentor*

You are not alone! In the United States alone, over 75 million people are caregivers, according to the National Alliance for Caregiving. Support groups can provide emotional support and great information to help you cope with caregiving. Searching for a mentor—someone who has been through the caregiving process—is another great idea. Walking in the footsteps of someone who has already been a caregiver can smooth your own journey.

Cure 5: *Ask For Help*

You don't have to care for your parents all by yourself. Delegate jobs to your siblings, ask your kids to help out around the house, and ask your husband to set aside some time for a date night. If you need more help caring for Mom and Dad and you or they can afford it, consider hiring outside help. Many people specialize in providing eldercare services and their help can be invaluable.

I had a hard time asking for help when I began caregiving for my parents. I wanted to manage everything myself and do it all my way. Before long, I was overwhelmed. My husband, Bob, realized this and asked, "Barb, what can I do for you?"

I blurted out the first job that popped into my head. "Grocery shopping!"

During all the years of our marriage, Bob had *never* been to the grocery store. But I needed his help so much—and he had been so sweet to offer—that I decided to make it work.

Usually my grocery list reads something like "Chicken, fruit, vegetables. . . ." I don't get too specific because I know what I want. But Bob wouldn't know. So, for his first trip to the store, I wrote down a precise list: "Half-pound of chicken breasts, one bunch of asparagus, box of strawberries. . . ."

When Bob returned from the store and placed the bags on the kitchen counter, he was so proud of himself. We started unpacking the bags. I pulled out the half-pound of chicken breasts. "Perfect!" I told Bob. He beamed, and admitted that he had asked advice from the butcher.

I kept unpacking. Instead of asparagus, Bob had picked out broccoli. Close enough, I told myself. It's green. But then I pulled out the strawberries.

They had been on sale. Bob loves a good sale.

He had purchased *three quarts* of strawberries. Three overflowing quarts of ripe red strawberries. Bob had no idea that strawberries only last for a few days. We spent the rest of the weekend eating strawberries with breakfast, lunch, and dinner. By Monday, we all had sores in our mouths. My refrigerator smelled like strawberries for a week. The kids refused to eat strawberries for the next three months.

A little voice in my head said, "See? You should just do the grocery shopping yourself." But I was smart enough to realize that getting everything exactly right wasn't worth it. Offering his help was the best gift that Bob could have given me, and my grateful acceptance was the best gift that I could have given him.

And you know what? Bob still goes to the grocery store every week. And I still thank him every time.

Ellen: A Caregiving Story

By Jim Berg

Taking care of my mother consumed me. I washed her clothes; I did her hair. I massaged her feet; I shaved her chin. And the odd part: I did it mostly for me. I hoped, among other things, that I might have one last chance to prove myself, to atone for my behavior as a teenager.

I knew my mom loved me; I never doubted that. But I'm not sure she liked me. I was sandwiched between two perfect sisters, smart and pretty, and I never felt that I measured up in my mother's eyes. I was the one who stayed out past curfew. I was the one who had a few drinks. I was the one who dabbled with drugs.

So I went regularly to visit her on Tuesdays and Thursdays at the nursing home, and I brought her to my house each Sunday. Mostly these were pleasant days. Some days she simply sat in her favorite chair and read while I did household chores; other days we sat together at the table and played cards. I especially enjoyed pulling out an old photo album and watching her smile as she paged through it, telling me stories I would never have heard otherwise.

Yes, mostly these days were pleasant. One Sunday, however, I remember with shame. I sat working through a stack of my mother's bills, frazzled with the accounting and the fact that I was sitting there on a beautiful afternoon, missing my daughter's softball game. I missed too many of them.

"It smells yummy," my mother said, referring to the warm cookies cooling in kitchen. And hinting, I knew, that she'd like one now.

"They just need a chance to cool," I said, focusing on the bills. "Then I'll get them."

"Just so they don't get too cool."

I looked over at her, sitting in the sunlight by the window with her feet propped up, a blanket pulled to her chin. I saw the impatience in her eyes and the tilt of her head, so I put my pen down, went to the kitchen and returned with warm cookies and milk. My mother took one bite and grimaced. "These aren't made from scratch," she said, shaking her jaw as though she had just tasted raw meat. As though I should be ashamed for trying to pawn off packaged cookie dough as homemade.

"No," I retorted. "I don't have time to make cookies from scratch because I'm always doing something for you." I grabbed the plate of cookies on the table at her side. "Right now," I said, "I'm missing Jill's game. I'm doing your bills. Ordering your meds and scheduling your appointments."

Her body deflated, it seemed, beneath the covers, and she turned her eyes to the floor. I felt terrible. Sick to my stomach. And I manufactured a quick smile to pretend I was kidding—but I had hurt her and it's a regret I'll always carry.

*****

One night while we were playing cards at the nursing home, I couldn't help myself and I asked her.

"Do you like me, Mom?"

She looked at me as though she didn't understand the question. "Do I like you?" she asked. "Of course, I like you. You're my beautiful daughter number two."

"Sometimes when I was young, I wasn't always so good to you."

"It was you," she said, touching my face, "that you weren't always so good to." I felt my face flush warm and tears welling up in my eyes. "I admired you," she continued. "Your independence."

Then my mother laid her cards on the table and smiled.

"Gin," she said.

*****

She's gone now and I find myself wondering what to do on a Sunday afternoon. I glance over at her empty chair, and I'm filled with sadness. Taking care of my mother did consume me—but it also healed me.

23

Stop, Look, and Listen—
Assess Mom's and Dad's Needs and Find Ways to Help

- **Learn how to assess your parents' needs**
- **Analyze the outcomes of your assessment to determine what kind of help Mom and Dad need**
- **Assist your parents with their challenges and ensure their safety**

After my parents moved into an apartment in an independent living facility, life got easier for them. She and Dad ate lunch and dinner at the facility's dining room on a daily basis, had regular housekeeping service, and no longer had to worry about household maintenance.

Then one day, I opened up their refrigerator and noticed stacks of Styrofoam take-home containers from the dining room. I grabbed one, lifted the lid, and discovered moldy leftovers. Feeling a little sick, I started peeking into each container in the fridge. Nearly every box contained weeks-old food. My mother had been bringing back leftovers and then ignoring them. This was unlike her. I took a good look around the apartment. Messy stacks of newspapers and magazines cluttered the floor. In the past, my mother had always kept a tidy house. Feeling uneasy, I checked the top drawer of their desk. I discovered several unpaid bills. The checkbook hadn't been balanced for months.

That's when I really started to worry. Clearly, Mom and Dad were struggling to live independently. And I had missed the signs. I hadn't noticed the changes in their lives for several reasons:

- **Denial.** I didn't want to admit that Mom and Dad weren't as capable as they used to be.
- **Respect.** I didn't want to intrude on their privacy or imply that they couldn't live independently.
- **Other demands.** My life was very hectic. I was taking care of my own family, my job, *and* my parents.

As I realized that they needed help, all sorts of questions popped into my head. What else had I missed? How many challenges was Mom facing? Was Dad facing similar issues? What needed to change? Would anyone in my family help me deal with this?

Once I took a deep breath and calmed down, I reminded myself that I had to *understand* the problems before I could solve them. I decided to **assess Mom's and Dad's needs** so I could figure out the best ways to help them. To learn what my parents' needs were, I had to look closely at how they were living. If I wanted to make their lives better and safer, I had to know what issues they were struggling with on a daily basis.

I was angry at myself for not noticing these changes earlier, but I also realized that I had a great opportunity to make my parents' lives better. Instead of attempting to caregive in the middle of a disaster, like I'd had to do when Dad was scammed out of $68,000, I could act *now* to provide solutions *before* a crisis arose.

Since this wasn't an emergency situation, I could gather information and work with my family to develop a plan, instead of haphazardly rushing to action. Rather than punishing myself for missing the signs of change, I concentrated on the fact that I could do something *now*.

NEEDS ASSESSMENT: The Basic Facts

What Is a Needs Assessment?

A *needs assessment* **is a series of checklists that evaluates your parents' current capabilities and helps you determine what actions and strategies will improve the quality and safety of their lives.** Using these checklists, you can figure out why your parents are struggling and what can be done to make life better for them. A thorough assessment examines the entire range of your parents' needs: physical, emotional, mental, and social.

Most parents want to stay in their own home for as long as possible. An assessment will reveal the benefits and shortcomings of their current living situation, and whether they can "age in place" successfully. For example, the assessment may show that Mom and Dad can stay in their home if some remodeling is done or certain kinds of outside help are hired.

In other cases, the assessment will confirm that your parents need to move into housing that provides more support. At first, Mom and Dad probably won't appreciate hearing that recommendation. But if you follow the assessment guidelines carefully, the results will give you an objective evaluation—facts that will make the unwelcome news easier for your parents and the rest of your family to accept.

You can assess your parents yourself or enlist the help of other family members. A professional with experience in eldercare—such as a social worker or geriatric care manager—can also be hired to perform assessments. If you expect family members to disagree about Mom and Dad's situation, hiring a professional to perform the assessment may reduce conflicts.

Checklists are an ideal way to gather information during an assessment. Checklists are objective and provide an easy way to record changes. They can also be designed to track change over a period of time. You can create your own checklists or use premade versions. This book has a **companion workbook** called *Before Things Fall Apart: The Essential Workbook on Caring for Mom and Dad*. You can find assessment checklists based on this chapter in the *Workbook*. Many websites and eldercare organizations also offer helpful lists. Checklist formats make it fairly simple to do an assessment, and once you get the process down, you'll find that future assessments can be done quite efficiently

Why Should I Assess My Parent's Needs?

Before I performed an assessment, I dealt with my parents' crises as they arose. I would devise a solution and then wait for the next problem to show up. I addressed Mom's and Dad's needs one at time, which prevented me from seeing the underlying causes of their problems. Anyone who does jigsaw puzzles knows that you can't get a sense of the whole puzzle from just a handful of pieces. But a complete assessment gave me *all* of the pieces, so that I could see the entire picture of my parents' lives. That way, I was able to spot the causes of their difficulties and find the best ways to help them.

When you meet with your siblings or other relatives to discuss your parents' needs, an assessment will help you to—

- **Generate an agenda**. An assessment gives you an objective list of Mom's and Dad's challenges.
- **Prioritize tasks**. An assessment helps determine what challenges need to be addressed immediately and in the future.
- **Reduce conflicts and disagreements**. An assessment generates objective information, rather than opinions or guesses.
- **Prevent emotions from derailing the family meeting**. An assessment provides clear facts that can help siblings who are struggling with denial or sadness about your parents' changing lives.

How Often Should I Conduct a Needs Assessment?

Your initial assessment provides a baseline that establishes your parents' status at that time. My first assessment took some time and effort, but subsequent assessments were less time-consuming because I already knew the process. In most cases, **updating the assessment twice a year** will be enough to keep you aware of changes in Mom's and Dad's lives.

Be aware that certain events may trigger changes that aggravate your parents' problems or spark a crisis. After one of these trigger events, update your needs assessment to track the effects of the incident. Assessment becomes particularly important after a trigger event because one or both of your parents may experience a sudden change in capabilities.

Here are some common triggers:

- New or suddenly worsening medical problems
- Release from a hospital and moving to a rehabilitation, assisted living, or skilled-nursing facility, instead of returning home
- Decline in the health of a spouse
- Death of a spouse
- Death of a pet

- Decrease in income
- A change of residence that results in a loss of contact with friends and/or family
- An event in their caregiver's life that changes the caregiver's focus and/or the time available for caregiving, such as the birth of a child or a medical problem

I remember an audience member at one of my speaking engagements who told me that while her father was in the hospital recovering from heart surgery, his girlfriend passed away and he never had a chance to grieve with her family. After her father returned home, he stopped going to his social club. "Then," the woman said, "my father's cat, an ever-present companion, died a few months later. I believe it was simply too much. He withdrew from the world completely. Being a long-distance caregiver, I didn't realize what was happening." This combination of triggers—his illness, the death of a close friend, the loss of socializing, and the death of a beloved pet—overwhelmed her father and shut him down physically, mentally, and emotionally.

If this caring daughter had known the benefits of performing an assessment after a trigger event, she might have discovered her father's problems more quickly and realized how to help him.

Am I Being Disrespectful by Assessing My Parents?

When you assess your parents, you are acting out of love and concern for their safety. This is entirely appropriate. You are not spying on them or trying to control them. In fact, each step of the assessment process requires that you spend quality time with your parents. Assessing your parents means learning more about them, seeing life from their perspective, and helping them in a loving way.

Many caregivers wonder if they should inform their parents of the assessment in advance. They don't know whether to sit down and discuss everything with Mom and Dad or quietly observe them and gather information before speaking to them. This is a valid concern.

Some parents will help you with the assessment by answering questions accurately and participating actively. Other parents will resist the assessment process. They may insist that they are completely capable. Or they may accuse you of judging them, and refuse to answer your questions honestly. In addition, once your parents know that you are observing them, they may become self-conscious and act differently, either purposely or unintentionally.

29

Your goal is to get the most accurate assessment. Take the approach that fits the situation best. For instance, you want Mom to be relaxed and natural when you assess her driving. If you announce that you are conducting an assessment, she will be self-conscious and may drive differently, so it is better to observe her without telling her about it. But if you suspect that Dad is not taking his blood pressure pills, opt for the direct approach and tell him that you need to sit down together and review all his medications right now.

I'm Not an Expert—How Can I Assess My Parents?

Assessing your parents doesn't require any complicated tools or specialized knowledge. You can easily remember these assessment strategies by thinking: **"A...E...I...O...You."**

- *A* **is for "Ask questions."** Talk to your parents. Asking questions helps you assess them in numerous ways and gives them an opportunity to share their worries and problems.
- *E* **is for "Enlist Neighbors/Others."** Give your telephone number to trusted individuals and ask them to call when they see *anything* that worries them about your parents. Your list of helpful third parties will include neighbors and friends, as well as professionals who work with your parents, such as their financial advisor, minister or rabbi, social worker, or home healthcare aide.
- *I* **is for "Inspect the home."** Look around your parents' home with a critical eye and note any changes.
- *O* **is for "Observe Mom and Dad."** When you spend time with Mom and Dad, pay attention to how they are talking, walking, and behaving. Ride as a passenger in their car.
- *YOU* **is for you, of course.** You are crucial to the assessment process. No one knows your parents better than you! Think of yourself as a detective who is collecting clues and interviewing people.

Who Can Help Me Assess My Parents?

Encourage siblings and other close family members to help with assessments. Share your assessment checklists with family members and ask them to record their observations when visiting Mom and Dad. When several family members participate in the assessment, they reduce the burden on the primary caregiver and provide fresh perspectives on the situation. Siblings who don't visit Mom and Dad on a regular basis can often spot changes more easily than a caregiver who sees them every day.

You may prefer to enlist the help of an expert to perform the assessment or to address the challenges facing your parents. Helpful references and services are listed in the back of this book. Here are the top resources for expert advice:

- **Geriatric Care Managers (GCMs)**. These professionals can help with assessments and may be hired as long-term overseers of Mom and Dad. Geriatric Care Managers are the "general contractors" of caregiving for your parents.
- **Certified Aging-in-Place Specialists (CAPs).** These professionals can advise you on modifying and remodeling your parents' home to improve safety, livability, and accessibility.
- **Your local branch of the National Association of Area Agencies on Aging**. This important national organization can help you locate resources and senior services available to caregivers and their parents in the parents' own community. The association also offers useful databases, including an Eldercare Locator and a Senior Housing Locator.

How Do I Perform a Needs Assessment?

When conducting a needs assessment, you will look at **nine critical aspects of your parents' lives**:

1. Finances
2. Personal Care
3. Transportation
4. General Health
5. Medications
6. Doctor Appointments
7. Memory
8. Emotional Status
9. Household Chores

Ready to Get Started?

The rest of this chapter will help you with assessing your parents' needs. The activities, checklists, and solutions are designed to help you understand the process and go through the steps. Depending on your parents' situations, you may want to conduct further evaluations too.

There is a three-step procedure for each of the nine areas of assessment:

1. **Assessment Activities.** Spend time with your parents while they perform particular tasks or routines. Observe their behavior and the condition of their home. Ask lots of questions.

2. **Assessment Checklists.** Record the results of your Assessment Activities using the checklists and/or written notes. Analyze the checklists to reveal the gaps between your parents' current situation and their ideal situation. Determine the causes of your parents' challenges. The checklists in the rest of this chapter provide good examples of useful questions. More extensive checklists are available in this book's companion, *The Essential Workbook for Caring for Mom and Dad.*

3. **Assessment Solutions.** Once you understand what Mom and Dad need, you can provide helpful solutions. Addressing your parents' needs will improve their lives, keep them safer, and help you minimize future crises. The remainder of this chapter offers some practical solutions to common problems. For more solutions, the Resources at the back of the book may also be useful.

THE NEEDS ASSESSMENT

FINANCES

ASSESSMENT ACTIVITY 1: **Sit down with your parents and observe them while they pay bills and engage in other activities related to money.**

For many parents, the first clear sign of cognitive problems involves finances. Mom and Dad may have difficulty paying bills, dealing with money-related issues, and making wise financial decisions. Many scammers know this and specifically target the elderly. Mishandling their money can have severe repercussions for your parents, so deal with financial issues *immediately*. If your parents don't have any cognitive challenges, this is the perfect time to set up a financial power of attorney so they will be protected later.

ASSESSMENT CHECKLIST—Finances

- Is the mail being opened regularly?
- Are your parents balancing the checkbook and paying the bills on time?
- Can they recognize dishonest business people and potential scams?
- Are you familiar with all the payees on their checks and credit card statements? Are there unexplained payments, new debts, or suspicious names?
- Are your parents engaged in any unwise financial practices such as compulsive gambling or compulsive shopping?
- Are they paying their taxes? Did they fill out their tax forms properly?
- If your parents use a computer, do they understand security issues such as phishing and viruses?

ASSESSMENT SOLUTIONS—Finances

- Establish a financial power of attorney while Mom and Dad are still mentally capable. This ensures that their money will continue to be managed properly even if circumstances change and they can no longer perform these tasks successfully themselves.
- Offer to become your parents' bookkeeper or sit down with them weekly or bimonthly to go through the mail, pay bills, and balance their checkbooks.
- Hire an accountant to handle their taxes.
- Help your parents avoid solicitations from charities, scam artists, and businesses by encouraging them to use their answering machine and/or caller ID to screen their telephone calls. Put your parents on the Do Not Call list.
- Protect your parents against identity theft. Warn them to *never* give out personal information, particularly their Social Security numbers and bank account numbers, to *anyone*.
- If your parents are computer users, instruct them on how to recognize Internet scams and potential viruses. Make sure that their security software is up to date, blocks pop-ups, and has a good spam filter.

PERSONAL CARE

<u>ASSESSMENT ACTIVITY 2:</u> **Visit your parents early in the day or stay overnight and observe their daily personal care routines.**

As your parents age, performing basic self-care tasks becomes more challenging. Poor eyesight or cataracts impair vision and make grooming more difficult. Parents with arthritis or memory issues may be unable to complete their nail and dental care routines. When reduced mobility or balance makes bathing a challenge, some parents try to make do with a swipe of a wet washcloth. Incontinence may go unnoticed or ignored, due to an impaired sense of smell, embarrassment, or the inability to bathe properly.

Even a task as simple as getting dressed can become a tremendous struggle. Arthritis or range-of-motion challenges can eliminate half of Mom's wardrobe simply because she can't put her clothes on easily. On top of all these challenges, fatigue or depression can sap your parents' interest in maintaining their appearance.

Bathing, teeth-brushing, nail care—these daily self-care routines help keep your parents healthy. Poor oral hygiene can lead to gum disease, difficulty in eating, and an increased risk of heart disease. If your parents can't clean their bodies effectively, then they may develop skin and urinary tract infections, which can lead to more serious medical problems.

Eating habits often change as people age, but their need for good nutrition remains the same. Your parents may not be eating properly due to a host of reasons. Medications, illness, dental issues, lack of social contact, a diminished sense of smell and taste, alcohol use, or depression can diminish appetite or discourage eating. While getting your parents to eat better can be a big challenge, the benefits are worth the effort.

ASSESSMENT CHECKLIST—Personal Care

- Can your parents safely use a bath or shower?
- Do they clean all body parts well? Are they using deodorant? Is Dad shaving?
- Can they use a toilet safely? Do they have any issues with incontinence?
- Do they brush their teeth well? How often do they brush their teeth? Are they caring properly for their dentures?
- Are they washing their hair and/or visiting a salon or barber regularly?
- Do they get dressed every day in clean clothes? Do they dress appropriately for the weather?
- Are they making unhealthy food choices? Eating irregular meals? Doing minimal food preparation?
- Have your parents lost weight?
- Do they look pale? Are they often tired?

ASSESSMENT SOLUTIONS—Personal Care

- Make showering and bathing easier and safer with modifications such as grab bars and shower seats.
- Add a seat raiser to the toilet.
- Brighten lighting and add task lighting to bathrooms and kitchens.
- Hire a home healthcare aide to assist with bathing and other personal care.
- Move the washer and dryer to the main floor to increase accessibility.
- Hire a laundry service or a housekeeper to help with the laundry.
- Pare down your parents' closets to provide a selection of seasonal clothing in good condition that can be mixed and matched, laundered easily, and put on with a minimum of effort.
- Stock the house with shampoo, toilet paper, laundry detergent, etc.
- Talk to your parents' doctors to determine if diminished appetite is a side effect of medication or a physical ailment.
- Make a list of the foods that appeal to your parents and keep the kitchen stocked.
- Sign them up for the Meals on Wheels program, which will supply one nutritious meal a day.
- Set aside extra servings when you cook at home, freeze them, and stock your parents' freezer.
- Hire a housekeeper who will do light cooking for your parents.

TRANSPORTATION

ASSESSMENT ACTIVITY 3: **Ride along as a passenger while your parent drives.**

Driving causes more conflicts between caregivers and their elderly parents than any other issue. You want to keep Mom and Dad safe and prevent them from injuring other people and damaging property. But Mom and Dad see driving as a hallmark of independence and can't imagine giving it up. Not being able to drive will be frustrating, inconvenient, and embarrassing for them. But if your parents aren't fully capable, driving puts them and others in physical and financial danger.

The best way to assess your parents' driving abilities is to ride along as a passenger while they drive. Observe them without being critical. You want them to reveal how they usually drive, not how they drive when someone is watching them.

Before you propose that Mom and Dad give up the keys, research alternatives such as public transportation, taxis, shuttles, or delivery services so that you can promote other transportation options. Don't insist that they stop driving without showing them how to be independent without a car. If your parents refuse to listen, then enlist the help of a third party such as their doctor, the DMV, their insurance agent, a geriatric care manager, or a trusted friend. The opinion of an expert or a friend can be very persuasive.

ASSESSMENT CHECKLIST—Transportation

- Do your parents get lost, even when driving to familiar places?
- Do Mom and Dad have trouble reading road signs or avoid driving at night?
- Do your parents show signs of slowed reaction time?
- Do your parents have trouble with complex maneuvers such as making a left-hand turn at a stop light when there are multiple lanes?
- Do Mom and Dad hear and react to emergency vehicles and warning honks from other cars?
- Do your parents see and react appropriately to bicyclists, pedestrians at crosswalks, cars pulling out from side streets and parking spaces, and other circumstances that depend on peripheral vision and alertness?
- Is anyone afraid to drive with your parents? Ask them why.
- Does your parents' car have new dents or scratches? Do your parents remember how the car was damaged?
- Have your parents' neighbors mentioned any driveway incidents, such as mailbox or trashcan damage due to your parents?
- Do your parents have any recent traffic violations?
- Have their auto insurance rates changed due to accidents?

ASSESSMENT SOLUTIONS—Transportation

- Encourage your parents to assess their own driving competency. They can get retested at the DMV, take a driving course from AARP or AAA, and/or ask their doctor's opinion.

- Work with your parents to set parameters for safer driving. Start with avoiding highways, bad weather conditions, driving after dark, and trips to unfamiliar locations. This is a good way to introduce the idea of driving less, which will make the decision to stop driving in the future easier.

- Introduce your parents to alternative forms of transportation. This can include taxicabs, buses, and rides from friends and family.

- Work with your parents to set a deadline for ceasing to drive, and hold them to it.

GENERAL HEALTH

ASSESSMENT ACTIVITY 4: **Observe your parents as they engage in everyday activities such as walking, driving, shopping, reading, and eating. Look for behaviors that indicate personal challenges.**

The state of your parents' physical health affects everything else in their lives. An assessment can help you diagnose an emerging or ongoing problem or address a relatively minor condition before the situation becomes more serious. Assessing general health involves observing your parents as they perform their daily activities, such as eating, walking, and watching television, and noting changes in their usual behavior. Enlist your parents' doctor and dentist to determine what these changes mean and how to deal with them.

According to *American Family Physician*, falls cause 70 percent of accidental deaths in people over 75 years of age. When a parent walks unsteadily or struggles to rise from a chair, they are at risk of falling. Because a fall can have such serious health repercussions, caregivers should address mobility issues as soon as possible.

ASSESSMENT CHECKLIST—General Health

- Does Mom or Dad have unexplained cuts or bruises that could have resulted from accidents or falls?
- Are your parents unstable when walking? Have there been changes in their gaits?
- Do your parents have difficulty getting into and out of cars, chairs, or their bed?
- Do your parents get dizzy when shifting between sitting and standing position?
- Can Mom and Dad get up and down the stairs safely?
- Are your parents disoriented or confused?
- Is your parent with diabetes taking the proper medications regularly and eating an appropriate diet?
- Does Mom or Dad struggle to read small print? Have trouble reading road signs when driving? Complain about not seeing clearly when driving at night or in the rain?
- Are your parents showing signs of hearing loss, such as turning up the television volume or missing words during a conversation?
- Do you parents have bad breath? Do they suffer from tooth pain or denture problems that interfere with eating?
- Do Mom and Dad experience insomnia? The average senior needs seven to nine hours of sleep a night—are your parents getting significantly more or less than that?

ASSESSMENT SOLUTIONS—General Health

If you are worried about Mom's or Dad's health, then **take your parent to the doctor or dentist to get a diagnosis immediately**. After you understand the medical issues and your parent receives treatment, you can make life better for your parents in many ways.

- Provide brighter lighting throughout the house, especially in bathrooms, kitchens, stairs, entries, and high-traffic areas.
- Make the bathroom more accessible and safer.
- Install railings on both walls of the stairways, add colored strips on the stair edges, and fasten a nonslip runner on the treads.
- Eliminate tripping hazards such as piles of books and magazines, electrical cords, carpet runners, and throw rugs.

- Encourage your parents to get exercise. Exercise improves balance, muscle strength, circulation, and appetite. Get them moving more by enrolling them in an exercise program, helping them purchase exercise equipment, introducing them to mall walking, buying them a Tai Chi DVD (and practicing with them!), or another similar strategy.
- Get your parents an emergency call button so they can immediately request assistance if they have a fall or accident.
- Purchase a phone with a loud volume control and large keypad.
- Initiate a discussion with your parents and your parents' doctor about hearing aids.
- Find large-print books or get your parents an e-reader with variable text sizes.
- Quiz your parents about the condition of their mouth and teeth. Ask about denture problems. Consult with a dentist as needed.

MEDICATIONS

ASSESSMENT ACTIVITY 5: **Find out if your parents are taking their medications properly.**

For your parents, taking their medications can be much more complicated than just popping a pill. If Mom or Dad takes several prescriptions, then remembering dosages, times, and possible interactions can be difficult. Even if your parents have excellent cognitive skills, dealing with multiple medicines can be challenging. **Taking medications properly is essential to your parents' health, so address this area immediately.**

ASSESSMENT CHECKLIST—Medications

- Do your parents take their medications at the proper times and in the proper dosages?
- Do they remember if and when they have taken their medications?
- Do they understand the purpose of each medication?
- Do they correctly order and refill their medications?

- Do they have the funds to pay for all of their medications?

ASSESSMENT SOLUTIONS—Medications

- Provide pill containers labeled with the days of the week or month to organize their medications. Some organizers include flashing lights or beeping sounds to alert users when to take their pills. Automatic medication dispensing devices are also available.
- Enlist the help of a reminder service that will contact them via phone, voice-mail, e-mail, or text. Reminder apps for cell phones are also available.
- Create a table or spreadsheet listing all of your parents' medications and show them how to record each time they take their medications.
- Hire or designate a person to organize your parents' medications on a weekly or monthly basis.
- If your parents take their medications incorrectly, refuse to take them, or forget to take them, then they need supervision. A nurse, hired companion, or you should oversee their medications. If cognitive issues are a significant concern, then moving to an assisted living facility should be considered.

DOCTOR APPOINTMENTS

<u>ASSESSMENT ACTIVITY 6:</u> **Go to doctor appointments with your parents.**

Most parents have some health concerns, and doctor appointments, medical tests, and treatments are a part of everyday life. Cognitive issues, even mild ones, can make functioning independently in a medical setting difficult. First, your parents must schedule, remember, and show up at their appointments. Second, they need to answer questions accurately, remember symptoms, conduct a sustained conversation with the doctor, understand diagnoses, remember instructions, and act on them. Due to the complex demands of this process, parents often need help in coping with medical appointments.

ASSESSMENT CHECKLIST—Doctor Appointments

- Can your parents schedule and remember to attend their appointments?
- Can your parents fill out their medical forms accurately and in a timely manner?
- Do your parents know their medical histories?
- Can your parents remember what they want to discuss, and can they engage in a productive conversation with the doctor?
- Are your parents familiar with all their medications and the directions for taking them?
- Do they understand the diagnosis, remember their doctor's instructions, and follow them properly?

ASSESSMENT SOLUTIONS—Doctor Appointments

- If your parents have serious difficulties with these tasks, then consider having them tested for cognitive issues.
- If you are not already listed on your parents' HIPAA forms, then ask your parents to add you. This will allow the doctors and nurses to share Mom's and Dad's medical information with you.
- Assist your parents with scheduling and attending their appointments. Possible tasks include calling the doctor's office, posting appointments on a large calendar, making reminder calls, helping with medical forms, and transporting your parents to the appointments.
- Accompany your parents in to their appointments to enable discussion, record the doctor's diagnoses and advice, and keep track of instructions, prescriptions, and treatments.
- Consider recording all or part of the doctor visit using an audio or video recording device. This allows you to give your full attention to the doctor and provides a record of the visit that can be reviewed later. This is especially helpful for a parent who may be forgetful or argumentative about the doctor's diagnosis or advice.
- Hire a Geriatric Care Manager or another supportive individual to help your parents with tasks related to medical appointments.

```
┌─────────────────────────────────────────────────────────────────────┐
│                                                                       │
│                            MEMORY                                     │
│                                                                       │
│  ASSESSMENT ACTIVITY 7:  Over the course of several visits or phone calls │
│  with your parents, ask questions and make requests that test their memories. │
│                                                                       │
└─────────────────────────────────────────────────────────────────────┘
```

It is time to assess your parents' cognitive health when they show signs of memory loss beyond occasional absentmindedness. Age, heart disease, high cholesterol, diabetes, and family history can all contribute to memory loss. According to the Alzheimer's Association, nearly 50 percent of Americans over age 85 have Alzheimer's disease, the most common form of dementia. As parents move into their 80s and 90s, some loss of cognitive function is not unusual.

You can get a feel for whether your parents' lapses of memory are serious by spending some time doing this Assessment Activity with them over several visits or phone calls. Here are some *activities* to probe your parents' memory skills during the visits or calls (use the *Assessment Checklist* to help you record your observations):

- Ask them about their opinions on a complicated issue or current event.
- Ask each parent to find a familiar object that is consistently kept in the same location.
- Assign each parent three consecutive tasks and observe whether they can retain the instructions and perform the tasks.
- Ask your parents to recall the foods they ate at lunch.
- Conduct a five-minute conversation and observe whether they can engage in a logical back-and-forth discussion or they wander off onto another topic.
- Discuss the past week's activities.
- Call or visit again the next day and review the conversation or activities to determine how much information they can recall.

ASSESSMENT CHECKLIST—Memory

- Do your parents remember dates, names, and appointments?
- Do they frequently struggle to recall the right word to use? Can they communicate their thoughts clearly?
- Do they remember where objects are located in the house?
- Do they perform repetitive movements or actions? Do they repeat certain phrases or questions again and again?
- Can they perform familiar tasks properly and follow directions?
- Can they interact successfully on the phone and take messages? Is their writing legible?
- Do they make repeated phone calls with no clear purpose?
- Can they use the oven, stove, and microwave safely, without risk of fire?
- Can your parents successfully follow a recipe?

ASSESSMENT SOLUTIONS—Memory

If you suspect that your parents are having cognitive issues:

- Ask your parents' physician to administer a Mini-Mental State Examination (MMSE). This short questionnaire can reveal cognitive impairment, particularly dementia. The test takes about ten minutes and can be repeated at each visit, allowing the doctor to monitor changes over time.
- If impairment is mild, devise ways to help your parents with challenging tasks. For example, set up an answering machine or voice mail to answer their telephone calls; dole out their medications into pill containers marked with the days of the week; make their appointments for them; and so forth.
- Assemble a team of professionals to help you with your parents' financial and legal matters, such as a financial planner and an eldercare attorney. Do this now!
- Provide mental stimulation by taking your parents on shopping trips, museum visits, out to lunch, to the bowling alley, or on other expeditions.
- Clean out their refrigerator on a regular basis. Make sure their food is fresh.
- Put labels on cabinets and drawers to help your parents identify the contents.

- Encourage your parents to place important objects consistently in a particular location, such as always putting their eyeglasses next to the night table lamp or the house keys in a bowl by the sink.
- Instruct your parents to let the answering machine pick up all their calls. Review the calls with them on a daily basis.
- Recognize that your parents should no longer be driving. Work with them on finding other transportation options.
- If they are forgetful, pull the knobs off the stove and remove items that could start fires, such as irons and space heaters, from the home. Buy appliances that have automatic shut-off features.
- Test all the smoke detectors and install fresh batteries on an annual schedule.
- If cognitive impairment is more serious, then moving your parents into an assisted-care facility may be the smartest, safest course of action. If parents with cognitive impairment come to live with you, safety-proof your house.

EMOTIONAL STATUS

ASSESSMENT ACTIVITY 8: Ask your parents specific questions about their emotions and activities. Watch for changes in emotions and behavior over time.

Your parents' emotional health is just as important as their physical health. Depression is a major problem for older adults, yet 90 percent of elderly people with depression are not diagnosed. Assessing your parents' emotional health can be tricky. You will need to ask questions and listen carefully, as well as pay attention to changes over time.

Asking "Are you feeling depressed?" is often useless, because your parents may be private about their feelings, worried about looking weak or "crazy," or simply unaware that they are depressed. Asking specific questions about your parents' lives is much more revealing. Instead, ask questions such as:

- What did you do for fun today?
- What did you eat for lunch?
- How are you sleeping?
- What are your plans for this week?

Parents who are struggling to live independently are at risk for anxiety and depression. When their capabilities decline and everyday tasks are more challenging, many parents become less physically active and less socially involved. This erodes verbal and social skills, as well as cognitive ability, and makes elders even less inclined to socialize or exercise. This downward spiral can destroy their quality of life and lead to depression. While caregivers often try to be respectful of their parents' independence, they need to be aware that this "independence" may eventually turn into unhealthy *isolation*.

ASSESSMENT CHECKLIST—Emotional Status

- Are your parents socializing and engaging in enjoyable or fulfilling activities, or are they avoiding activities they once enjoyed? Do they avoid leaving the house?
- Do Mom and Dad eat healthy meals on a regular basis, or have they lost interest in food?
- Do your parents get an appropriate amount of sleep each night? According to the NIH, seniors should sleep an average of seven to nine hours a night. Do your parents sleep more than that? Or do they have insomnia?
- Has one or both parents experienced a marked change in mood or personality? Does Mom or Dad have mood swings? Crying jags?
- Are your parents anxious or worrying excessively?
- Are they sad all the time?
- Is either parent becoming increasingly suspicious or paranoid?
- Is Mom or Dad expressing increased irritability or anger?
- Are your parents engaging in unusual behaviors such as hoarding, inappropriate clothing choices, compulsions, repetitive actions, wandering, or hallucinations?

ASSESSMENT SOLUTIONS—Emotional Status

These solutions are designed to boost your parents' emotional health. If you suspect that either of your parents is depressed, consult with their physician.

- Increase your parents' social contact by encouraging them to attend events at their local senior center, social club, or house of worship.
- Enthusiastically promote regular exercise for them. Be a role model!
- Bring their old friends over for a visit or take your parents and their friends out to lunch.
- Suggest that your parents pursue new hobbies or revisit old ones.
- Provide them with a list of interesting local volunteer opportunities.
- Give your parents coupons or gift certificates to their favorite area restaurants.
- Hire a companion to spend time with your parents every day or several times a week.
- Purchase season tickets to arts or sporting events for your parents.

Important Note: If you suspect that one or both of your parents are *depressed*, get a specific diagnosis from an internist or gerontologist. Treatable ailments such as urinary tract infections, dehydration, malnutrition, certain vitamin deficiencies, or an under-active thyroid can produce symptoms that mimic depression. If your parent is diagnosed with depression, please treat this condition as seriously as any other medical issue.

If you suspect that one or both parents are showing the early signs of *dementia or other cognitive issues*, go back and work through **Assessment Activity 7: Memory**.

HOUSEHOLD CHORES

<u>ASSESSMENT ACTIVITY 9:</u> **Over the course of your next few visits to your parents' home, actively observe the condition of their house, both inside and out.**

Changes in the condition of your parents' home can reveal changes in their physical, mental, and emotional health. If your parents have kept a well-maintained, tidy home in the past but have recently become neglectful, investigate further. There is a reason for their change in behavior. Mom and Dad may be physically unable to keep up with the chores, or depression could be sapping their energy and interest in maintaining a clean house. If they have cataracts, they may not even see the stains, or your parents may be embarrassed because the stains are due to incontinence. Stacks of newspapers, magazines, or mail on the floor need to be removed as a safety hazard and are a possible sign of diminished cognitive capability. Keeping track of annual household maintenance jobs can also be difficult if your parents are experiencing memory issues. Performing the jobs may have become too difficult or dangerous for your parents if they aren't in good physical shape.

ASSESSMENT CHECKLIST—Household Chores

- Are the kitchen and bathrooms clean and tidy?
- Have your parents been dusting and vacuuming regularly?
- Do they regularly collect their trash from around the house and put it out for pick-up?
- Do they regularly go shopping for their groceries and other needs?
- Are the refrigerator and pantry well-stocked? Is there expired or old food?
- Are the cleaning supplies stocked and accessible?
- Are unexplained stains appearing on carpeting, furniture, or bed linens?
- Is there excess clutter or signs of hoarding?

- What is the condition of the yard? Is it being mowed and maintained regularly?
- Is the home's exterior well-maintained?
- Are the sidewalks clear of bushes, leaves, snow, etc.?
- Is there evidence of insects or vermin in the house?

ASSESSMENT SOLUTIONS—Household Chores

- Hire a housekeeper, gardener, and/or maintenance person to assist your parents.
- Make chores easier by buying a self-propelled vacuum, easy-start mower, or appliances that are easier to use.
- Take your parents to the doctor to determine if they are experiencing any loss of vision, hearing, cognitive ability, or if they are dealing with depression or unusual anxiety.
- Begin discussing alternative housing options with your parents if maintaining a house has become overwhelming for them.

I've Completed the Needs Assessment . . . What's Next, Barbara?

First of all . . . congratulations! Completing the needs assessment is a huge achievement. Now you have the caregiving tools to help your parents face their challenges now and in the future.

The next step? Build your caregiving team. Talk to Mom and Dad about what they need and want. Then sit down with your whole family to discuss the best ways to help your parents and how to share the responsibilities of caregiving. When you, your siblings, and your parents work as a team, you can accomplish so much, and succeed together.

Checking In

By Jim Berg

I cross the river on the way to my father's condo. It's fall and the color in the trees is truly stunning. Reds, yellows, and oranges flutter in the air, competing for attention like little kids at a family gathering, a last brilliant hurrah before the drab of gray skies and bone-chilling temperatures.

When he opens the door, I give him a quick hug and notice the stubble on his chin. I see a blanket rumpled on the floor. "You sleep on the couch again?" I ask.

"Must have dozed off," he replies, his eyes rimmed with red.

Dirty dishes are piled in the sink and scattered across the table.

"Hasn't Elsie been in to clean?"

"I fired her." He looks away from my gaze. "Kept moving my stuff around. I couldn't find anything."

I sigh. I brew a pot of coffee and check his refrigerator to see what he's been eating and what he's been ignoring. I smell the milk. It's still good. Then I sort through his mail and pay the bills.

"I thought Brenda was coming today," he says.

"She is," I say, "Later. She'll be here at three to take you to the doctor." I point to a calendar on the wall. "It's all right there for you."

He walks to the calendar and stands there with one hand on a chair for support. "Yup, there it is," he says, studying the calendar as though it holds a secret he can't quite grasp.

*****

The stubble on his face is not a good sign. I suspect that he never went a day in his adult life without shaving until recently. And driving back over the bridge, I'm overcome with a sudden memory: My father chasing me through the house like Frankenstein, his feet thumping ominously on the floor, his arms straight out from his body, sweeping me up in his embrace and giving me a whisker rub while I squeal in delight.

The memory is bittersweet. I feel on the verge of understanding something—something important—but it is without shape and it eludes me. I watch the fall colors moving in the wind; I watch a lone sailboat cut through the water below me. And I feel his scratchy stubble warm against my face.

I Love You and I Want to Help You—
Have Those Important Conversations with Mom and Dad

- **Have conversations about the seven most important issues facing your parents**
- **Prepare yourself and your parents for a good conversation**
- **Modify your conversations for physically or mentally challenged parents**
- **Change your strategy when your parents say "No"**

Although we spend our whole lives talking, we still have trouble *communicating.* I was reminded of this when one of my good friends told me a story about taking her Mom to get a passport photo.

My friend and her mother stopped by a drugstore with a photo department that offered passport photos. A young female employee quickly set up a white background screen and grabbed a camera. Then she instructed my friend's mother: "Stand in front of the screen and we'll take your picture." My friend's mother complied, but instead of facing forward, she turned around and stood with her back to the camera, looking expectantly at the white background screen.

My friend was perplexed. "Mom stood there, and stood there, and stood there. . . . At first I thought she was composing her face. The photographer, a young gal, had no idea how to handle this. Finally, I spoke up and told her, 'Uh, Mom, you need to turn and face the camera'."

Her mother quickly turned around and the photo was snapped. Once they left the drugstore, the two sat in the car in the parking lot and laughed uproariously. Her mother couldn't explain her actions.

After puzzling over the incident for a few days, my friend realized that the word "screen" had created the confusion. She remembered that her mother had recently learned how to video-conference with her grandchildren on the computer. Video-conferencing requires the user to face the computer *screen* in order for the computer's tiny camera to capture an image. When confronted with the pharmacy's white background screen, her mother must have assumed that it was just like her computer screen. So she obediently faced the background screen and waited to have her picture taken. And, my friend recalls, "The girl did tell her to stand in *front* of the screen. She didn't say, 'Please face the camera'!"

Communicating with your parents is an essential part of caregiving. Yet, accomplishing this can be surprisingly difficult. My friend's mother found herself in a new situation and did her best to follow directions. She still ended up facing the wrong direction. When you try to talk to your parents about important issues, they may get confused and "face the wrong direction" for many reasons. Physical and cognitive challenges. Fear. Anger. Embarrassment. Lack of knowledge. As a caregiver, you need to find ways around these barriers.

Having productive conversations with your parents is essential because no matter how close you are to your mother and father, you can't read their minds. You can't make decisions based only on your feelings or someone else's advice. You can't assume you know what your parents really want and need. You have to *ask* them. This chapter will provide you with strategies for making communication easier, clearer, and more effective.

Here are the **seven most important topics to discuss with your parents**:

- Medical and financial documents
- Coping with everyday life
- Health issues
- Housing alternatives
- Finances
- When to stop driving
- End-of-life wishes

You may look at this list and think, "Ugh. I don't want to talk about *any* of this with Mom and Dad." Be aware that **postponing these conversations is the number one mistake** made by my audiences and readers. They can't figure out how to start talking about such touchy matters. And they tell themselves that there will be plenty of time to discuss these topics—in the future. They procrastinate until it is too late.

Recently, a couple in their 40s came to one of my presentations. The next morning, the husband left for an out-of-town business trip. He got a call from his wife that evening. She opened with, "Well, I've got some good news and some bad news. The good news is that we heard Barbara McVicker speak last night. The bad news is that Mom just had a stroke."

This couple attended my presentation to prepare for the future, when they would be caregivers for their parents. They had not imagined that their "future" would begin the very next day.

If your parents are in good health, this is the *perfect* time to talk. You aren't stressed by a crisis and your parents are at their best, cognitively and physically. In my ideal world, everyone would **sit down with Mom and Dad on their 70th birthdays,** eat some cake, and start planning for the future.

No one wants to ask Mom, "If your heart stops beating when you're dying in the nursing home, should they resuscitate you?" No one wants to tell Dad, "You've got to stop driving before someone gets hurt." As families, we're much more accustomed to talking about the best way to cook the Thanksgiving turkey or arguing over which team will win the Super Bowl. We're good at that. Talking about the important issues is uncomfortable and much trickier. You need to prepare yourself for this task.

I'm going to help you. Talking effectively with your parents takes patience and planning. A sense of humor always helps, too. You'll have to invest some time and effort, but the results will be worth it. In the end, everyone will feel safer, more in control, and less anxious about the future.

Step 1: *Plant the Idea*

No one likes to be ambushed. If you suddenly bring up a tough topic with no warning, you can't expect your parents to react well. Here are three ways to start them thinking:

- **The Conversational Approach.** Present the topic and then step back and let your parents initiate the conversation. Bring up the topic several more times over the next few days or weeks. *"I just updated my will. Do you think you and Dad need to do that?"* If this doesn't work, be more direct: *"Your lives have changed a lot since you made out your wills 20 years ago. They need to be updated. Let's take 15 minutes to talk about that right now."*

- **The Written Approach.** Give your parents a chance to educate themselves before you have a conversation. You can use books, magazines, pamphlets, websites . . . whatever will catch your parents' attention. *"Here's an article with lots of good ideas about how to make your bathroom safer. Please take a look at this, and we'll talk about it tomorrow."*

- **The Third-Party Approach.** It's hard to shrug off the advice of an expert or trusted advisor. Choose a professional who your Mom and Dad respect, such as a financial advisor, a physician, an elder law attorney, or their minister or rabbi. Encourage your parents to meet with a third party. Sometimes, hitching a small task to the larger issue makes the visit less daunting. *"It's time to go in for your flu shot again. Let's take that opportunity to get your physical out of the way,"* or *"I'm working on my own financial plan. Let's get together and do yours too, so everyone is on the same page."*

Step 2: *Do Some Prep Work*

As Alexander Graham Bell once said, "Before anything else, preparation is the key to success." If you were going to give a speech to a group of strangers, you would do research, write notes, and rehearse. Treat Mom and Dad like an important audience, too. Before you speak to them, prepare yourself. Here are some important steps:

- **Do your research.** Knowledge is power, and being well-informed makes you feel more confident. You will also be more helpful to your parents.

- **Remember that Mom and Dad are your audience.** You know your parents well. Adapt your approach to their personalities and problem-solving methods. Are your parents optimistic or pessimistic? Outgoing or withdrawn? Resilient or easily wounded? Take a few moments to imagine how they perceive their situation. Empathy is a very powerful tool.

- **Assess your parents' needs *before* you start a conversation.** Conduct a thorough Needs Assessment (see **Chapter 2: Stop, Look, and Listen**) so you have a clear idea of your parents' capabilities and limitations. Doing a Needs Assessment will give you *facts*, which will help you bring objectivity and evidence to an emotional discussion.
- **Include siblings if you think their participation will make the discussion more constructive.** Seeing all of their children gathered around the kitchen table impresses most parents. They will take the conversation more seriously. If possible, meet with your brothers and sisters before sitting down with Mom and Dad. You can update your siblings on your parents' current situation (especially if you have done a Needs Assessment). You can also give them an opportunity to discuss *their* future responsibilities to Mom and Dad.

   Every family member should play a role in caregiving. According to a 2009 study by the National Alliance for Caregiving, only one out of ten adult children caregivers feels that the caregiving burden is equally split among their siblings. A word of caution, though: during times of stress, old resentments and sibling rivalries nearly always resurface. For more advice on dealing with your brothers and sisters, take a look at **Chapter 4: We're All in This Together.**

Step 3: *Prepare Yourself Emotionally*

Nothing short-circuits a conversation faster than emotional outbursts on both sides. Your parents may become upset, angry, or confused. This is normal. Try not to mirror those emotions. I know how difficult it can be to maintain a positive attitude in this situation, but if you become emotional too, everyone will stop focusing on the intended topic. Here are some strategies for keeping the conversation on track:

- **Be patient and stay calm.** I've placed this first on the list because being patient and calm will help you attain all the other positive behaviors listed here. As an added benefit, your serenity will reduce the anxiety of other family members.

- **Be reassuring and supportive.** You want to honor your parents' wishes while keeping them safe and healthy. Let Mom and Dad know that they are not alone and you will always love them and care for them.
- **Be kind but firm.** Try to decide in advance how much you can help your parents in terms of time, effort, money, and emotional support. Be clear about these boundaries to prevent miscommunication. Mom or Dad may act demanding, pushy, angry, or frightened. Instead of responding to their emotions, *stay calm*. Resist being manipulated by guilt or aggression. Listen to your parents and do your best to follow their wishes, but also recognize that you may need to disagree on some points. Reaching a consensus may be impossible. Remember that responsible caregiving for your parents may require choosing what is best for them, even when they clearly want something different.
- **Be prepared for negativity.** Remember, your mother and father are facing many losses. They are in a period of transition, and transition can be difficult and frightening. Their negativity may be the byproduct of their fears.
- **Don't be distracted by drama.** If your parents try to deflect the conversation by bringing up a different issue, guide the discussion back to your original point. If Mom and Dad get angry, again *stay calm*. They may unconsciously provoke or try to upset you as a way of deflecting or controlling the conversation.
- **Do not put up with verbal abuse.** If your parents become abusive or aggressively refuse to cooperate, you should step back and say, "I love you, but I do not deserve this. I will come back tomorrow. I am leaving now." *Breathe* to reduce your stress, detach from today's conversation, and walk away for now. Then try again another day soon.

Step 4: *Start Off on the Right Foot*

Give yourself and your parents the benefit of beginning the conversation in the best possible way. Here are some pointers for how to do that:

- **Plan to talk in person, not over the phone.** You want your parents to be fully engaged in the conversation, not distracted. Your physical presence is very important. Fifty-five percent of communication comes from body language.

58

- **Wait for a quiet, peaceful time without distractions.** This is particularly important if your parents have hearing difficulties or dementia. For instance, a Fourth of July barbecue with kids, dogs, food, beer, and loud conversation is not an ideal venue.
- **Pick one topic.** Don't try to cover every topic suggested in this book with your parents in one evening. You will overwhelm and exhaust them and not resolve anything.
- **Start on a positive note.** Thank your parents for sitting down with you to talk about this important topic. Be cheerful.
- **Express heartfelt emotions.** Tell Mom and Dad that you are initiating this conversation because "I love you and you love me. You raised me to be a trustworthy and honorable child, and I have your best interests at heart. You deserve my respect . . . and you have my respect."
- **Use stories to get people talking**. A story can be a low-key, nonthreatening way to begin a discussion. Talking about someone else's problems lets you approach an uncomfortable topic indirectly. Scour the newspaper or TV for examples. Nine caregivers shared their stories with me for my first book, ***Stuck in the Middle: Shared Stories and Tips on Caring for Mom and Dad***. You might use one of those stories to begin a discussion with your own parents.

Step 5: *Talk the Talk*

Talking to your parents is an essential part of caregiving and requires you to be aware of what you say and how you say it. To make your conversations more effective, keep the following suggestions in mind when talking with Mom and Dad:

- **Go slowly.** Don't rush the conversation or issue orders. Give your parents time to think, answer your questions, and ask questions of their own.
- **Be a good listener.** Pay attention and make it clear that you are listening to your mother and father and understand what they are saying. Repeat back their words so they know you have heard them correctly.
- **Have a two-sided conversation**. You probably have some great ideas and lots of good information. It will be hard to resist the temptation to lecture or issue ultimatums, especially if the conversation is moving slowly or Mom and Dad are resisting the issue.

Take a deep breath, focus on your parents, and respond to their questions in small bites. You cannot hurry these discussions.

- **Look at the bigger picture.** Ask your parents about their goals, their fears, their concerns, and their wishes. These kinds of questions encourage people to think about their long-term plans. Here are some examples: *"If you had to use a wheelchair to get around, how would that change things?" "If you broke your hip and needed to go to a rehabilitation center, where would you like to go?"*

- **Look at the whole family, not just one or two people.** Often, parents are so preoccupied with their own challenges that they don't see the big picture. Remind Mom and Dad that you must consider the needs of the entire family. Work together to devise a plan that benefits everyone—your spouse, your other siblings, and the grandkids. For example, you might say, *"Mom, you've said you don't need to go to assisted living because I can help you with cooking and cleaning every day. But I have to take care of my own family, too. Instead, I would love to be able to visit you and just sit and enjoy your company. We could do that if you lived in an assisted living apartment."*

- **Be specific, not vague.** If you want to know what Mom and Dad are thinking, ask very specific questions that require specific answers. Instead of, "What do you think about retirement communities?" ask questions such as, *"Have you visited Lakeside Groves? Let's go together next Thursday. We can even try out the dining room at no charge."* The promise of a free meal would motivate Dad to go almost anywhere!

- **Offer options.** Your parents, like everyone else, need to have choices to maintain their sense of independence. Offer several options when Mom or Dad must give up a privilege or responsibility, such as driving or housework. For example, say *"Dad, you've got to stop driving at night because of your cataracts. But there are some great alternatives that will still get you where you want to go. You can hire a cab, call your grandson, or take community transportation. Let's try these out together."*

- **Use "I" statements.** Communication experts often talk about how "you" statements are too accusatory: *"Mom, you haven't paid your bills in a month!"* Rephrase these sentences using "I" statements, such as, *"I'm worried about your bills, Mom. I saw an overdue notice for the mortgage. Can we sit down together and get caught up?"* Other helpful phrases: "I wish . . ." and "I feel. . . ."

- **Use facts to support your statements.** It's hard to argue with science and math. When Dad complains that taking a cab will cost too much money, you can remind him that owning a car means maintenance, gas, and insurance. If he has an accident, he will have to pay for towing and repairs and his insurance rates may go up. Even if he spends $50 a week on cab fare, that only adds up to $2600 a year. Twelve months of car payments, insurance, and upkeep will cost much more than that.

- **Engage in therapeutic fibbing.** Occasionally, it will be smarter and more expedient to tell a white lie when you want to help and protect your parent in a loving way. For years, my diabetic mother ignored her health problems. She didn't monitor her blood sugar or take her insulin regularly. The staff at her independent living community recommended a move to an assisted living facility, but Mom refused.

When she was 87 years old, a medical crisis sent Mom to the hospital. Her doctor prescribed rehabilitation after her release. I told Mom that, in order to receive rehab treatment, she needed to move temporarily into an assisted living facility. In reality, I knew that her stay in assisted living would be permanent. Within a few months, Mom was much healthier and happier than she had been before her medical crisis. While living at the assisted living facility, Mom had made friends and become comfortable with her new situation, and she stopped asking about her apartment.

- **Don't overdo it.** If the discussion starts to get too difficult, if your parents are too negative, or if you find yourself arguing with them . . . Stop! Take a break, step back, and start the conversation later at a better time.

- **Be persistent.** Resolving an issue may take more than one conversation.

- **End on a positive note.** With your parents listening, verbally review all that you have accomplished, and make sure that your written notes make sense to you and are accurate. Thank and praise your parents for wrestling with this difficult issue. Then enjoy a fun activity together.

Step 6: *Don't Be Afraid of Their Fears (or Yours)*

The best way to get rid of fear? Talk about it!

If you can get Mom and Dad to talk openly about their concerns, everyone benefits. Many older parents stagger along under a heavy load of fear. Talking will help release that tension. And once your parents confess their anxieties, you have the opportunity to address their concerns using sympathy and information.

Here are some things your parents may worry about:

- Moving to a new place
- Having enough money to live on for the rest of their lives
- Losing their independence
- Being a burden to their children
- Losing their physical or mental abilities
- Getting sick or developing dementia
- Dying

Share your own fears and feelings. You must have concerns about your own future as well as your job as caregiver. To help your parents see the whole picture, talk about how caregiving impacts you, your independence, your own family, and your career.

Step 7: *Unpack the Emotional Baggage*

In a perfect world, you would sit down with your parents and have a loving, rational discussion that allows you to settle on satisfactory solutions. But we are imperfect creatures. There are a handful of **powerful emotional roadblocks that can impede or stop discussion**. Consider whether you face any of the following challenges:

- **Deep-Seated Beliefs and Attitudes.** Your parents aren't going to change (at least, not very much). If they have grown up with dearly held religious or cultural beliefs, then you aren't going to budge their world view. They may believe that the oldest daughter must always take in her elderly parents. Or they may be convinced that being a burden on their family is unacceptable. Your parents may even shut you out of the conversation because they do not want to involve you in issues they consider private.

62

Strategy: Make certain that you understand your parents' beliefs and attitudes so you can talk effectively with them. You don't need to agree with them to understand how they think.

- **Misconceptions and Outdated Ideas about Growing Older.** Your mother and father may have been caregivers for their own parents. That experience can strongly influence their outlooks on both caregiving and growing older. Years ago, however, people often didn't live long enough to develop chronic illnesses. Your parents might envision caregiving as a few months of intensive nursing. Nowadays, caregiving may mean *years* of care.

The quality and variety of housing available to older adults today is impressive. Many older people do not realize this and your parents may fear that leaving their home means moving into a squalid "old people's home." Urban legends, such as the story about the family that lured Grandma into the car by telling her she was headed for the beauty salon and then dumped her at the nursing home instead, can add to your parents' anxieties.

Strategy: Facts dispel fears. Fight your parents' misconceptions with good information. Visit local continuing care retirement communities and assisted living facilities to educate yourself on the latest options available to Mom and Dad. Learn about services and transportation options that can help them live longer in their own home, too.

- **Codependency.** One or both of your parents may not be able to function independently. In some marriages, one spouse takes care of almost everything. If the capable spouse deteriorates or dies first, the remaining partner has difficulty functioning alone. Some parents also exhibit "learned helplessness." They act overwhelmed and helpless, forcing their caregivers to do nearly everything for them. Despite the appearance of dependency, these parents are exerting unfair control over the caregiver.

Strategy: Conduct a Needs Assessment (see **Chapter 2: Stop, Look, and Listen**) to determine what your parents are capable of doing independently. If they are capable, step back and stop doing some of these tasks. Let them assume these responsibilities again. This is mentally and physically healthy for them—and you.

- **A Difficult Past.** Caregiving can be a risky venture when your family history includes issues such as alcoholism, emotional or physical abuse, drug problems, grudges, or estrangement. Don't fool yourself into thinking that the situation will be easier or better because you are an adult. Family relationships rarely improve during a time of crisis. Assuming that everything will be better is not sunny optimism. It's another version of denial.

  Strategies: People in this situation need special tools for caregiving. I recommend using what I call the *Three T's*:
  - *Thoughtfulness*. Be conscious of your own need, be considerate to yourself, and pay close attention to how you react to your parents.
  - *Therapy*. Don't rule out seeking professional guidance when dealing with emotional baggage. A good therapist or a well-written book addressing your family issues can be invaluable.
  - *Third Party*. Be realistic about what you can or cannot do for your parents. Taking on the responsibilities of caregiving may not be right for you. The healthiest path for everyone involved may be to find other people to care for your parents. This may mean hiring outside help (skilled or unskilled), or working from a distance with an attorney or healthcare professional.

Step 8: *Dealing with Especially Challenging Circumstances*

Your parents may have physical or mental limitations that complicate your conversations with them. They may struggle with poor vision, hearing loss, memory loss, confusion, or other issues that prevent them from easily engaging in conversation. Your relationship with your parents may have emotional limitations as well. For example, you may be caring for them out of a sense of duty rather than love. Or they may create emotional roadblocks that prevent your conversations from moving forward. Don't let factors like these stop you from trying to engage them in important conversations. Make your best effort.

I'm going to offer you some pointers for dealing with issues that complicate productive conversations with your parents.

Communicating with parents with vision or hearing impairments presents special challenges. Here are some tips:

- Be patient.
- Choose a distraction-free location for your conversation.
- Get down to eye-level with them, whether they are in bed, seated, or in a wheelchair.
- Make sure you are in their hearing and visual range.
- Look them straight in the eye.
- Exaggerate your facial expressions so they see the big smile on your face.
- Use big gestures to keep their attention.
- Put a hand on their arm, or place both hands on their shoulders. This physical connection helps them focus their attention and shows that, even though you are talking about difficult things, you are also saying, "Mom, I have a connection with you."

Talking to parents with dementia is even more demanding. All of the above tips are very helpful. Try to incorporate the following suggestions, as well:

- Speak slowly and clearly.
- Take your time. Don't rush.
- Repeat yourself often.
- Keep everything simple.
- Offer only one or two choices. Five housing options will overwhelm your parents and make them anxious. Narrow the field down to the best one or two choices.
- Focus on your parents' feelings, not the facts. Your father may not be able to verbalize his thoughts clearly, but you can pick up clues from his behavior. Let him know you understand through your actions and words, such as *"Dad, I can see that you are upset,"* or *"This seems to be bothering you. Let's come back to this topic later."*

You've Done All You Can . . . and Your Parents Still Say "NO!"

What can you do when your parents refuse to discuss issues about their future? Here are some tried and true strategies:

- **Call in the cavalry**. Ask your siblings or other family members to join the discussion. This can be a sticky situation, because you don't want your parents to feel as if their children are ganging up on them. At the same time, the sincere concern of three or four people can have a powerful effect. Be sure to establish ground rules before having a group discussion. For example, everyone gets a chance to speak in turn, and no one is allowed to interrupt when someone else is speaking.
- **Ask directly for your parents' cooperation.** Tell your parents that you are overwhelmed and need their help and understanding. Assure them that you don't want to dump a load of guilt on them, but also explain the impact that caregiving is having on your life. Be very clear that if you don't make time to take better care of yourself, you soon won't be able to care for anyone—including them.
- **Pull out your secret weapon . . . start crying.** Tears can be very effective, especially if you feel overwhelmed and frustrated. A crying son or daughter makes such a powerful impression that your parents may choose compliance. Most parents do not want to see their child hurting.
- **Bring in hired guns.** When all else fails, call in the outside resources available. Social workers, your parents' attorney, doctors, ministers or rabbis, and trusted family friends may have better luck talking to your parents. Geriatric care managers can be hired by the hour for assessments or to help present options. Elder mediators are trained to help family members overcome their conflicts and move forward.
- **Accept reality.** Your adult parents have a right to say "No," even when they are making a bad choice. If your parents are truly incapable and pose a danger to themselves or others, you can turn to state authorities for help in establishing a guardianship.

How About You?

Don't wait. Open up a dialogue with your own kids now. Discuss **your** wishes concerning housing, driving, end-of-life medical directives, and other important topics. Opening up the lines of communication and having these conversations *now* is a priceless gift of love and respect to your children.

Throwing Dirt

By Jim Berg

It was a cold, snowy day: gray skies, blackbirds cawing in the barren trees, the grass brown and matted. He bent down and clawed dirt out of the side of the hole, crumbling it in his hand and sprinkling it over her casket.

He stared at the dirt under his fingernails, and he remembered the first time he had been at the site and his mother had stood alongside of him. His father had refused to join them, but she insisted that they see the gravestone together nonetheless.

That had been a gray, cold morning, too, with a farmer picking corn in the field to the south, the ears of corn heavy, bending the brittle-white stalks to the ground. He remembered it vividly: the wind shaking the trees, her arm wrapped around his waist, the sparkling brown of her eyes.

"I guess," she said, "I just wanted to be here once standing and not lying."

He smiled, and they stood there with the wind ruffling their jackets and kicking up dirt and scattering leaves across the ground.

We're All in This Together—
Use the Family Meeting to Create a Caregiving Plan

- **Schedule and prepare for a family meeting**
- **Determine the role you can play in caregiving**
- **Hold a family meeting to decide on a caregiving plan**
- **Delegate responsibilities and plan the next meeting**

For my first book, *Stuck in the Middle: Shared Stories and Tips for Caring for Mom and Dad*, I collected the experiences of real-life caregivers. I learned that every family handles the job of caregiving in its own way. In the final chapter, a woman named Amelia tells the story of how her family worked together to care for their mother.

As "Momma" got older, Amelia and her four siblings "tag-teamed" the caregiving work. At first, Amelia's youngest brother moved into their mother's home to provide daily support, while Amelia cooked Momma's meals and hired an in-home healthcare provider, and another brother helped with the finances. When their mother's health worsened, Amelia and her older brother searched exhaustively until they found the ideal facility. After Momma moved there, family members visited every day. "We'd drop in at all hours. Literally. Just to check. To see what was going on," recalls Amelia. At the end of their mother's life, says Amelia, the siblings continued to work together: "We didn't do anything overly invasive or unnecessary for Momma, but we did things to keep her here." Amelia's family communicated so well that they maintained a sense of peace and unity, even through the most difficult times.

We all aspire to have a family like Amelia's family. But sibling relationships can be tricky even under the best circumstances. When the time comes to care for Mom and Dad, the situation becomes even more challenging. In fact, caregivers with siblings often tell me that they would rather be "only" children. They wish that they didn't have to face the arguments, compromises, and drama involved in sharing the caregiving duties. On the other hand, caregivers with no siblings often long for a brother or sister to help them. They would love to have a companion to share the work and the worries. There is no perfect situation. During caregiving, family members will be both a source of stress . . . and a source of strength.

Your family should expect to have conflicts during caregiving. This is normal! Even strong families can become dysfunctional during this stressful time. You and your siblings are probably struggling with feelings such as these:

- Long-established family dynamics dating back to childhood
- Guilt and confusion over the role-reversal with your parents
- Grief over seeing your parents grow less capable and less independent

Mom and Dad can also add to the confusion. Comedian Paul Reiser has a great quote about this. He says, "The reason our parents can always push our buttons is because they were the ones that installed them!" Family dynamics during caregiving are so complex that writer Francine Russo compiled an *entire book* dealing with caregiving and families, entitled *They're Your Parents, Too!: How Siblings Can Survive Their Parents' Aging without Driving Each Other Crazy.*

But here's the honest truth about caregiving: **you cannot do it alone.** And you should not try. When your parents reach a point where they need help and support, you and your siblings (or other involved relatives) must communicate efficiently and constructively in order to take the best possible care of your aging parents.

Family meetings are a great tool for reducing conflicts and enabling family members to create a successful caregiving plan. The concept of a family meeting is simple: bring together the members of your immediate family to deal with caregiving issues. During these meetings, your family will do these critical activities:

- Discuss your parents' current status.
- Decide how to help your parents.
- Distribute responsibilities.
- Plan for the future.

Family meetings are essential to maintaining healthy relationships within families during the caregiving process. Instead of talking to individual family members in a disorganized fashion, you can improve communications by providing a structured setting where everyone can participate. **I'm going to give you clear goals and established rules for a family meeting** to help all of you stay on task and generate solutions. Without establishing goals and rules, your discussions will meander, irritate, produce no results, and might even cause destructive rifts.

Effective family meetings can achieve all of these positive outcomes:

- Diminish conflicts and tensions.
- Improve communication.
- Allow everyone to share the responsibilities of caring for Mom and Dad.
- Prevent caregiver burn-out.
- Strengthen family relationships.

Caring for your parents is a part of your adult life. It is not a responsibility to be avoided or a burden to be borne alone. For you and your siblings, caregiving for Mom and Dad is an essential part of your family history. All of you together can chose to make this a dark chapter, or you can decide to create a story about cooperation, communication, and love.

Assess Before You Leap

Assessment Step 1: *Get the Facts about How Mom and Dad Are Doing*

Assessing your parents' needs is the first step in preparing for a family meeting. A thorough needs assessment of your parents' situation will help your family chart a course of action and plan for the future. This assessment can be conducted by you and your family members or by a professional such as a geriatric care manager, social worker, or in-home healthcare provider.

If you anticipate disagreements or denial from your siblings or parents, hiring a professional can be very helpful. An expert evaluation helps prevent disputes, because the information is impartial. Unlike a family member, a third party can't be accused of taking sides, holding grudges, or avoiding reality.

For more information on assessing your parents' needs, see **Chapter 2**.

A needs assessment will give you the following vital information:

- Reveal the specific challenges facing your parents.
- Determine the types of help they may need.
- Highlight the issues that require immediate attention.
- Help your family to prioritize the caregiving tasks.
- Provide the basis for a workable long-term plan.

Assessment Step 2: *Take a Good Look at Yourself*

Mom and Dad aren't the only ones who need an assessment. Before the meeting, you need to examine your own expectations and limits as a caregiver. Determine your needs, your capabilities, and the demands on your time. If you are the person initiating the family meeting, then there's a good chance you have already decided to volunteer to be the primary caregiver. If so, you need to accurately determine how much time, effort, and money you can contribute to your parents' current and future care.

People often underestimate the demands of caregiving. Keep in mind that the caregiving period often lasts longer than expected. Your parents may require ten or more years of support and attention. The experience is also physically, emotionally, and financially challenging. In addition, once you assume the role of primary caregiver, it is difficult to withdraw from that position.

The number one problem for primary caregivers is their tendency to take on too much responsibility. Remember that your siblings will appreciate knowing which jobs *you* can reasonably perform and which tasks need *their* attention. Establishing these expectations in the beginning will benefit everyone.

Caregiving makes significant demands on all aspects of your life:

- **Family and Home.** Caregiving for your parents requires a lot of time. You will have less energy and time to spend with your immediate family. Can the members of your own family assume more responsibility for caring for themselves and the home? Will you need to hire outside help?

- **Career.** If your job is demanding, you may not be able to function at the same high level. You will probably need to take time off to take your parents to doctors' appointments and to carry out other caregiving duties. How do you expect caregiving to impact your finances, job status, and retirement benefits?

- **Finances.** On average, adult children caregivers spend at least $5500 a year to help support Mom and Dad, according to a 2007 study by Evercare and the National Alliance for Caregiving. How much can you reasonably contribute towards your parents' care?

- **Health.** Can you handle the physical and mental demands of caregiving without significantly impairing your own health? Do you take good care of yourself?

- **Emotional state.** Caregiving is difficult, even when you are emotionally healthy and stable. If you are undergoing your own emotional struggles or have a negative relationship with your parents, caregiving can be incredibly challenging. Do you have positive strategies for dealing with emotional stress—counseling, recreation, exercise, and so forth?

Assessment Step 3: *Get Your Own Family Involved*

Caregiving for your parents also places demands on the members of your immediate family. According to a national survey done by Caring.com, 80 percent of the respondents felt that caregiving placed a strain on their marriage. Good communication helps to ease these stresses.

Sit down and talk with your spouse. Talk with your kids if they are old enough to understand. Clearly explain your parents' situation and how you hope to help them. Ask for your family's assistance with household chores and responsibilities. Encourage your spouse and children to express their concerns. Take their opinions seriously. Actively listening to your family members will help you see the situation from their perspective.

Assessment Step 4: *Suggest That Your Siblings Talk with Their Families Too*

If you do have siblings, ask them to consider how participating in caregiving will affect their own families, careers, homes, health, finances, as well as how geographic distance may impact their participation. The goal is to have everyone honestly assess their situations. Siblings who have thoughtfully considered these issues will be well-equipped to participate in a family meeting because they understand their own abilities and limitations.

Lay the Groundwork: Preparing for a Family Meeting

Groundwork Step 1: *Decide Who Will Attend*

Throughout this chapter, I refer to "you and your siblings" when discussing the family meeting. For many families, this is accurate. For others, the definition of "family" is more expansive. Your children, your spouse, or other close family members may play important roles in caregiving. Depending on your family, the list may include aunts, uncles, cousins, grandchildren, or friends. If someone is going to be closely involved in caregiving for your parents, then that person should probably join the family meeting.

Before the first meeting, decide whether your parents should be included. If Mom and Dad are physically healthy, mentally capable, and emotionally stable, they may be in a great position to lead the meeting themselves. In this case, introduce your parents to the concept of a family meeting about caregiving. Your parents will probably be surprised or hesitant. They may insist that "It's too early to talk about that!" Explain that making decisions *now* will have benefits for everyone later. For your parents, creating their own plan for the future gives them control and peace of mind. For you and your siblings, having a plan will reduce conflicts and make caregiving much easier. Encourage your parents to read this chapter and offer to help them plan the meeting.

If your parents struggle with physical or cognitive issues and need help right now, hold your first family meeting without them. If your parents are confused or in pain, then involving them in complicated discussions is unfair. They will be overwhelmed. Instead, take the initiative and arrange for a family meeting on your own. You and your siblings need to hammer out a caregiving plan for the present and the future. This plan will be the goal of your first family meeting.

74

Holding an initial meeting *without* Mom and Dad will allow you and your siblings to accomplish the following:

- Talk honestly about the challenges facing your parents.
- Iron out sibling conflicts without placing your parents in the middle.
- Discuss a wide range of possible solutions without confusing or frightening your parents.
- Design a caregiving plan that works for everyone.
- Agree on an agenda for a meeting with your parents.

After you and your siblings have settled on a basic plan, then sit down and talk to your parents. By that time, you will have a clear idea of the most important issues to discuss with them. See **Chapter 3: I Love You and I Want to Help You** for advice on how to have effective, constructive discussions with your parents.

Groundwork Step 2: *Schedule the Meeting*

Contact your siblings to arrange the meeting. Try to choose a mutually convenient time and location. Ideally, everyone will physically meet in the same place. If this is impossible due to your siblings' commitments or locations, plan for the absent person to be involved via speakerphone or video-chat. Let your siblings know the goals of the meeting in advance. Do not be vague and do not plan to "surprise" your siblings. Tell them exactly what will be happening. Your family should not feel ambushed when they show up for this meeting.

Plan for a maximum of two hours. Cramming everything into one session is potentially destructive. Your family should expect to have more meetings (tell them this ahead of time). Resist the temptation to try to cover everything at the first meeting, because your focus and productivity will diminish after two hours. Marathon meetings also provoke conflict as family members grow fatigued and irritated.

If possible, plan a fun family activity after the meeting. Nothing too complicated. A dinner, a movie, a walk, or a friendly basketball game are possible options. Something as simple as a good film on DVD and some popcorn can provide a positive ending to a stressful afternoon.

Groundwork Step 3: *Design an Agenda*

The goal of the first family meeting is to design a caregiving plan. If you have done a complete needs assessment of your parents, then you will have a detailed list of the challenges facing your parents. The assessment will also reveal what types of support are needed and which tasks have the highest priority. Use the information in the assessment to generate an agenda for the family meetings. Place the *most urgent concerns* at the top of the agenda to ensure that they will be addressed in the first meeting.

Areas where your parents may require help include these:

- Personal care
- Household chores and meals
- Transportation
- Doctors' appointments and medications
- Finances
- Emotional support
- Legal matters

Groundwork Step 4: *Share and Edit the Agenda*

Send out the agenda and the needs assessment to all family members attending the meeting. Tell them that suggestions for modifying or reshuffling the agenda are welcome, but must be made before the meeting. Edit the agenda if necessary, send it out again, and let everyone know that this plan *will not* be modified during the meeting unless an unexpected change in your parents' situation reshuffles the priorities. Taking this no-nonsense approach to the agenda will help your family stay on track and accomplish more during the meeting.

Groundwork Step 5: *Recommend Sources of Helpful Information*

Your parents may have specific challenges, such as bathroom safety issues or Alzheimer's disease. Direct your siblings to information on these. If everyone arrives at the meeting well-informed, then your family members will accomplish more. You and your siblings will also feel more confident when making decisions. I've included a **list of potential resources** at the end of this book.

Cool, Calm, and Collected: Holding the Family Meeting
Meeting Step 1: *Use "Barbara's Rules of Order"*

Caregiving for Mom and Dad is an emotional topic. Even if you have the most understanding siblings in the world and anticipate nothing but smiles and hugs, you still need to provide some rules for discussion. Share these rules with your siblings at the beginning of the meeting, before you start through the agenda.

Rule 1: Stick to the agenda. Following a pre-set agenda will keep the meeting from wandering onto other topics or getting derailed by emotion and conflict. If anyone purposely or inadvertently jumps ahead or veers off the topic, then gently bring them back on course.

Rule 2: Take turns. Go around the table in an orderly manner and give each person a chance to speak. Do not interrupt them. If your family struggles with this idea, bring a small keepsake to the meeting. This item can be something significant, such as a little framed photo of your parents, or silly, such as a stuffed animal. Explain that while a speaker has the object, other members of the family must not interrupt that person. Their concerns can be discussed later. Once the speaker is finished, the keepsake is passed to the next family member. The physical object silently reminds everyone to take turns and be respectful.

Rule 3: Speak for yourself. Ask everyone to use "I" when speaking and to avoid using "you." A statement that begins with "you" can feel like an accusation or criticism, which isn't constructive. This rule can be challenging for some people but will reduce conflict.

Rule 4: Respect your parents. Your family will probably be discussing personal information about your parents. Even if Mom and Dad are not sitting at the table, you should be respectful. Remind yourself that, as long as your parents are mentally competent, you are *not* making the decisions for them. Instead, you are trying to help them make *their own* decisions.

Rule 5: Listen to others. Pay attention when your family members are speaking. If you anticipate that any family member will dominate the discussion by being long-winded, then set a maximum speaking time. You can even bring and use a stopwatch, if that will help.

Meeting Step 2: *Designate a Secretary*

Ask a family member to volunteer to take down notes during the meeting and record the family's decisions. This person will also have the job of sending copies of the notes to everyone after the meeting.

Meeting Step 3: *State the Goal of the Meeting*

Even if the goal is obvious since everyone has an agenda, repeating these words has power. Reminding everyone of the goal at the same time also reminds your family members that they have agreed to work together to accomplish an important job.

Meeting Step 4: *Limit Reminiscing, Socializing, and Sharing of Feelings*

It's understandable if you and your siblings need time to reconnect, tell stories, or discuss their issues, feelings, and anxieties. **Your family should definitely take the time to do this, but keep those activities** *separate from your family meetings.* The main goal of the family meeting is to create a caregiving plan. Everything else should be done at another time.

Meeting Step 5: *Move through the Agenda*

Discuss the challenges facing your parents in the order presented on the agenda. As a family, make decisions about how to address these challenges. Agendas for a family meeting commonly include the following goals:

- Create a list of tasks requiring the most immediate attention.
- Design a caregiving plan. See more about this below.
- Identify issues you need more information about.
- Assign tasks to individual family members.
- Decide what topics to discuss at the next meeting.

Meeting Step 6: *Design a Caregiving Plan*

You and your siblings are now a caregiving team, working together to help your parents. Before your family starts assigning individual tasks, choose a general caregiving plan. Once you and your siblings have settled on a caregiving plan, delegating responsibilities becomes easier.

You have four basic options for how to approach the tasks of caregiving:

Option A: One Primary Caregiver. Under this plan, one family member handles the majority of the caregiving duties while receiving support from the secondary caregivers. According to a study by the National Alliance for Caregiving , 43 percent of primary caregivers feel that they have no choice in assuming this demanding role. If one sibling becomes the primary caregiver, then other family members need to be both appreciative and proactive in their support. Having a primary caregiver does *not* relieve other family members of caregiving responsibilities.

Option B: Rotating Caregivers. Just as the name suggests, this option designates one family member as the primary caregiver for a specific period of time. After that, the job passes to another family member. In some cases, for example, Mom and Dad will actually move from one caregiver's home to another on a predetermined schedule.

Option C: Shared Caregiving. In this caregiving plan, family members distribute responsibilities as evenly as possible. Each caregiver will have a list of tasks. For example, in a two-sibling family, one caregiver might handle appointments, finances, medications, and legal concerns, while the other caregiver provides support with day-to-day needs such as bathing, clothing, household chores, meals, transportation, and social activities.

Option D: Geriatric Care Manager. If none of these caregiving arrangements work for your family, consider hiring professional assistance. Geriatric care managers are eldercare experts who perform needs assessments, make recommendations, access resources, and advocate for elderly clients. Hiring a geriatric care manager can eliminate many family conflicts and provide your parents with great professional care. As an added bonus, Mom and Dad may be more willing to listen to a professional expert. Some long-term care insurance policies provide for a geriatric care manager.

Meeting Step 7: *Share the Duties*

Once your family has settled on a caregiving plan, divide up the specific responsibilities. Your assessment will have provided you with a list of the tasks that need to be done to keep Mom and Dad healthy and safe, both now and in the future. Each sibling or family member should review the list of tasks and then offer to take responsibility for the jobs that they feel best qualified to handle. If you are lucky, the tasks will distribute themselves evenly. If not, any remaining tasks should be fairly divided.

Each family member should leave the meeting with a list of tasks to accomplish. No one should get a pass due to their busy career, kids, or geographical distance. *Everyone* is responsible for helping your parents. Family members who cannot assume fair portions of the responsibilities can contribute money, respite care, or some other form of support.

Meeting Step 8: *Support the Primary Caregiver*

Secondary caregivers must provide support and encouragement to the primary caregiver. A well-supported caregiver will be healthier—physically, mentally, and emotionally—and better able to do the hard work of caregiving. Support is a way of showing gratitude, and family members who provide support will feel more involved and less guilty.

When I was the primary caregiver for my parents, my sister had a habit of phoning me to thank me and tell me, "Everything you are doing is great." Just hearing this helped keep me going. As I slogged through those difficult years, my sister constantly encouraged me and listened to me. Most importantly, she served as my safety valve, letting me vent my anger and frustration without criticizing me. Her support helped me to survive and prevented burnout and bitterness.

Here are ways that your family can support the primary caregiver:

- Check in by phone or e-mail on a regular basis and ask, "How are **you** doing?"
- Provide respite care by caring for Mom and Dad while the primary caregiver takes a much-needed break.
- Offer to take on your sibling's least-favorite task.
- Express your thanks often.

- Be sympathetic and encouraging to the primary caregiver
- Avoid being critical or bossy.
- Send thoughtful little gifts.
- Hire and pay for outside help.

Meeting Step 9: *Deal with Conflicts*

You and your siblings should expect to have conflicts. Some are situational, due to the stresses and challenges of caregiving. Other conflicts will be personal and may be so entrenched in old family dynamics that everyone has a hard time getting through the family meetings.

If conflicts disrupt the meeting process so dramatically that your family can't move forward and accomplish the tasks necessary for successful caregiving, then consider asking for professional advice. Bringing in an impartial third party, such as a mediator, social worker, or clergy person, can be extremely helpful.

Meeting Step 10: *End the Family Meeting Effectively*

Allocate 15 minutes at the end of each meeting to review accomplishments and confirm your family's plan. Do not be concerned if this meeting did not address everything on the agenda. Simply roll these issues over into the agenda for the next meeting.

During the last 15 minutes of the meeting, do the following:

- Praise the group as a whole.
- Review the topics that were discussed.
- Restate the decisions that were reached.
- Record the list of tasks that need to be done before the next meeting. Make sure everyone has something to do, including research.
- Outline what the agenda will be for the next meeting.
- Ask everyone to pull out their calendars. Set up a date, time, and location for the next meeting.

Meeting Step 11: *Send Out a Summary*

Within a few days of the meeting, the family member who volunteered to be the designated secretary should share the meeting notes and the details of your family's caregiving plan with all attendees. The plan should include these items:

- A statement of each family member's role in the caregiving plan
- The separate lists of specific tasks paired to each family member
- A timeline of future caregiving tasks, if your family had time to address this
- The date, time, and location of the next meeting

The Next Big Hurdle: Meeting with Mom and Dad

When you and your siblings feel ready, set up a meeting that includes Mom and Dad. Let your parents know what will be discussed. This may be a very difficult time for them, especially if they are already struggling with the loss of their capabilities and their independence. Reread **Chapter 3**, which covers communications with your parents. Share the chapter with your siblings.

Depending on your parents' capabilities, adapt the meeting structure to suit Mom and Dad. Here are some suggestions:

- Limit the agenda. Do not try to discuss or solve every issue at once.
- Keep the meeting short. One hour or less should be sufficient.
- Take turns talking to your parents. Only one person should be speaking to them at any time. This will reduce confusion and prevent your parents from feeling as if their children are "ganging up" on them.
- Provide choices that work. When Mom and Dad have a big decision to make, such as moving to assisted living or hiring an in-home healthcare aide, do the research for them. Explore the options, identify the best choices, and discard the rest. Then, when you present your parents with two or three great options, they can make a well-informed choice without becoming overwhelmed or frustrated.

Keep Up the Good Work: Continuing to Meet

Good communication is essential to good caregiving. Continue to hold family meetings throughout the caregiving process. These meetings will help you and your siblings stay organized and informed. Caregiving responsibilities will be shared more fairly and Mom and Dad will receive better care. Regular meetings will also help you maintain healthy and supportive relationships with your siblings. Caregiving is a marathon, not a sprint, so make these meetings a regular part of your life.

Remember, too, that communication can come in many forms. For example, when you find a helpful article on caregiving, e-mail it to your siblings. If you are the primary caregiver, then take photos or videos of Mom and Dad and send them to your siblings. A Facebook page for your family is another good way to share information, stories, and updates.

One of my favorite family communication stories came to me from a teller at my local bank. She told me that after reading my first book, ***Stuck in the Middle***, she inscribed the names of her eight brothers and sisters on the inside of the front cover. She then mailed the book to the first sibling on the list, asking him to read the book, check off his name, and pass it on to the next family member. My book made its way across the United States, hopscotching from home to home, until it returned to Columbus. "That way," she told me, "I knew that we were all on the same page."

I love this story, because my bank teller understood exactly what good communication can do for a family. **When family members are "all on the same page," they make the very best caregiving team!**

Sitting round the coffee table, in our parents' living room
Grown children, our feelings weren't the best
We'd lost Daddy in November, now Mama in June
Years of caring for the dying had put us to the test
Long hours by their bedsides, we'd all done too much
None sure the others had done quite enough
For the ones we loved

But if they'd been there, they would have told us
 Hold hands with each other, kiss and make up
 Find some forgiveness in your hearts, you're all you've got
 That's what they would have said to us . . . if they'd been there

There was a box there on the table, we'd not noticed it before
Left by neighbors, the way that Mom had planned
It was filled with old love letters they'd written in the war
Our eyes were filled with tears as we read with trembling hands
How Mama'd tell Daddy each cute thing we'd say
Poems he wrote about us, our hearts were touched that day
By the ones we loved

 And if they'd been there, they would have told us
 Hold hands with each other, kiss and make up
 Find some forgiveness in your hearts, you're all you've got
 That's what they would have said to us . . . if they'd been there

And the love they had lived, lived once more in that room

Like when were children, we knew what to do

And if they'd been there, they would have seen us

Hold hands with each other, kiss and make up

New understanding in our hearts, we're all we've got

Mom and Daddy would have been so proud of us . . .

If they'd been there . . . if they'd been there

"If They'd Been There"

By: Karen Taylor-Good, Annette Cotter, & Roberta Schiller

Don't Wait!—

Help Organize Mom's and Dad's Five Essential Documents

Assist your parents with—

- **Making decisions about end-of-life care**
- **Creating or updating their Wills and Trusts**
- **Designating trusted people to make medical, financial, and business decisions in case your parents are unable to make these decisions**
- **Adding your name to their HIPAA Privacy Authorization Forms**

Everyone groans when I start talking about the five essential types of legal documents. Yet **these documents have a tremendous impact on you and your parents**. When properly executed, the five essential documents will protect your parents medically and financially, ensure that their estates are properly handled, and help you to provide Mom and Dad with the best care.

The five most important documents to consider are these:

1. **Living Will**
2. **Health Care Power of Attorney**
3. **Health Insurance Portability and Accountability Act of 1996 (HIPAA) Privacy forms**
4. **Last Will and Testament**
5. **Financial Power of Attorney**

If your parents have already completed, signed, notarized, and stored these documents, then you are very fortunate. In my experience, however, it is unlikely that your mother and father have all their legal paperwork in perfect order.

Many people avoid dealing with these documents because they feel intimidated or overwhelmed. This chapter offers a starting point for you and your parents. Depending on your parents' needs, they may or may not require all five documents. Consider the ways in which these documents can help your family and then consult with a professional in order to make the appropriate decisions.

Start Talking Now

If Mom and Dad don't have these documents, then you need to fix that. Right now.

Almost everyone waits until a crisis to start thinking about this, which can be disastrous. Your parents must be mentally capable in order to approve these forms. By waiting, your family is simply rolling the dice and hoping that Mom and Dad won't have any health problems that compromise their judgment. **Waiting is a gamble with no payoff.**

Taking care of these documents now will save time and money in the future. Your parents will also prevent family conflicts by making their wishes clear while their mental clarity is not in question. In addition, you will feel better knowing that all the necessary paperwork is in order and stored in a secure place. So will your parents.

Sounds good, doesn't it? Yet, many caregivers procrastinate or completely avoid dealing with these documents. Trying to talk to parents about money, illness, and death isn't easy. You have my sympathy. But I can't overstress the importance of getting these papers in order.

If you are still hesitating, consider the case of Terri Schiavo, which was in the news a number of years ago. At age 26, Terri suffered a heart attack and severe brain damage, and remained in a persistent vegetative state for 15 years. For seven of those years, her husband battled her parents for the right to withdraw her feeding tube, which would result in her death. Her husband insisted that Terri had informed him that she did not want her life prolonged if she ever ended up in a coma. But Terri never told anyone else or wrote down her wishes. Her parents wanted to keep her alive. The conflict between Terri's husband and parents developed into an international debate over end-of-life decisions that eventually involved the U.S. Congress, the first President Bush, and the Vatican.

Terri was young and she hadn't anticipated needing any of the important documents that could have helped her family. You and your parents don't have this excuse. In fact, no one really does. Right now, you have an excellent opportunity to involve all three generations of your family in conversations about end-of-life issues and make sure that *everyone's* documents are in order.

Why Don't Mom and Dad Want to Talk?

When you bring up topics relating to money and death, your parents may try to change the subject. They may resist sharing financial information. They may respond with phrases such as, "It's in bad taste to talk about money," or "That's my private business," or "Why are you so interested in *my* money?" Try not to be insulted if a raised eyebrow or suspicious glance accompanies this last question.

Fear or superstition may prevent Mom and Dad from talking about illness and end-of-life plans. Many parents find these topics uncomfortable or disturbing. Others simply look at the list of five documents, don't know where to start, and immediately throw up their arms in defeat.

I like to tell a story about Bob Hope, who lived a few months past his 100th birthday. When Bob was on the verge of death, his family and friends gathered around his bed. As they told him how much they loved him and would miss him, someone asked, "Can you tell us where you want to be buried?"

Without missing a beat, Bob answered, "Surprise me!"

With all due respect to Mr. Hope . . . it was a little late to be making end-of-life decisions.

Set the Wheels in Motion

I am going to be *pushy* about this—**you need to take care of these matters *now*.** In order for your parents to approve these documents, they must be intellectually capable and in good mental health. Set yourself a deadline for getting all five documents filled out, signed, notarized, and safely filed away. Pick a deadline that will get you going and keep you moving, but don't wait any longer than a year to get this done.

I admit that when I became a caregiver for my parents, I didn't want to deal with paperwork, lawyers, and my parents' indecisiveness. The job felt huge. But I took small bites, working away at these necessary tasks bit by bit. I found that much of the work, such as talking to my parents and educating myself about the different documents, could be done in advance of meeting with an attorney.

My mother and father did not want to talk about illness, death, and money. Yours probably won't be eager to discuss these topics either. To spur my parents into action, I encouraged them to "do the right thing," instead of trying to push them. I like to call it "positive enabling."

If your parents are avoiding discussing their essential documents, here are a few suggestions:

- **Be a good role model**. Go to your lawyer, get your own documents in order, and then tell your parents that your lawyer would like to look at their papers "to see how their plans flow into yours."
- **Select the right lawyer**. Choose someone who will make your parents comfortable. Or hire a different lawyer for each parent, if that works better.
- **Pay for the lawyer yourself**. If Mom and Dad are concerned about costs or don't want to impose on you, tell them that you've already paid the law firm to review their documents as part of your own financial planning. I took this route because I knew that paying now would save me money and heartache later.
- **Mention the grandchildren**. A Will makes it easy to leave money and keepsakes to the kids.
- **Point out the benefits**. A Will allows Mom and Dad to control the fate of their money and property. If they die without Wills, the courts will make the decisions.
- **Appeal to their sense of thrift**. Point out that a Will protects their assets, and Uncle Sam will claim a larger chunk if they don't have one. This one really motivated my parents!
- **Bring in a third party**. Estate planners, attorneys, and doctors (for medical/HIPAA documents) can be very helpful. Advice from an authority figure can carry a lot of weight, and your parents may feel more comfortable talking to an outsider about personal issues.

Please keep in mind that I am *not* an attorney or a healthcare professional. I am only providing you with helpful information, not legal or medical advice. To create the five essential documents, you must contact the proper legal, financial, and medical professionals.

Do Your Homework

Before your parents meet with an attorney, perform a few tasks that will make the process go more smoothly. Here are the most important ones to do:

- **Locate any existing documents** and make certain they are filled out correctly. Examine the documents to determine if any need to be updated. Organize them so you can find what you need, especially in an emergency. Keep a set of photocopies too, just in case.
- **Make appointments with trusted professionals** who can help with this process, such as attorneys, doctors, and financial advisors.
- **Educate yourself**. The rest of this chapter will provide you with more information about these documents.
- **Visit the attorney beforehand** and establish a relationship. Then ask the attorney what your parents need to do before they meet with the attorney.
- **Talk to your parents** about their end-of-life wishes. Jot down notes as they talk.
- **Explain the benefits of having a Health Care Power of Attorney and a Financial Power of Attorney** to your parents. Encourage them to select a first and second choice for each position.
- **Ask your parents to list their assets**, especially if they have never prepared Wills before. Then ask them to choose the people and charities that will inherit their estate. They also need to select an executor, who will be in charge of carrying out the instructions in the Will. If their assets have changed over the years, work with your parents to update their assets list and Wills.
- **Ask Mom and Dad if they would like you to accompany them to the attorney's office.**

What You Need to Know about the Five Essential Documents

1. Medical Documents

The three most important *medical* documents are the Living Will, the Health Care Power of Attorney, and HIPAA Privacy Law forms. These documents are written instructions from the patient (your parent) to their doctors about medical care. Update these documents every two to three years, especially if your parents' state of residence, marital status, or health changes. Powers of Attorney must also be updated if your parents want to change the persons designated on these forms.

Living Will

A Living Will expresses the patient's wishes concerning life-sustaining measures, including extraordinary medical treatments such as feeding tubes and ventilators. By the end-of-life stage, 76 percent of people will be unable to participate in some or all decisions, according to an analysis of the University of Michigan Health and Retirement Study in the *New England Journal of Medicine*. The Living Will is designed to speak for patients who can no longer express their own wishes due to terminal illness, imminent death, coma, or a persistent vegetative state. Your parents can choose the types of medical care that are acceptable or not acceptable to them in these situations.

For example, if your father does not want to be intubated, he can indicate that choice in his Living Will. The terms of the Living Will should be very specific and tailored to the patient's medical conditions. Your parents may worry that this document will deny them the option of changing their minds during a crisis. Put Mom and Dad at ease by assuring them that they can verbally alter *any* part of their Living Will at *any* point during treatment by talking to their attending doctor or healthcare provider.

Requirements for the Living Will vary from state to state. In many areas, the state medical association has adopted a standardized Living Will form that will be instantly familiar to healthcare professionals in that state. Investigate this possibility yourself or discuss the form with your parents' attorneys.

When your parents design their Living Wills, they may want to consider adding a **Do Not Resuscitate Order (DNR)** to their medical documents. The DNR states that resuscitation should not be attempted when a person suffers cardiac or respiratory arrest. This document complements the Living Will by giving more specific information about end-of-life medical procedures.

Most people don't realize that cardiopulmonary resuscitation (CPR) has a very poor rate of success for the elderly and those with multiple medical conditions. According to bioethicist Viki Kind, CPR is successful only 17 percent of the time for *healthy* patients. In cases of serious illness, the rate of success drops dramatically—sometimes all the way to zero. Resuscitation attempts can result in broken ribs, invasive procedures, terrible stress, and disorientation. Your parents need to think hard about their end-of-life wishes.

Health Care Power of Attorney

This document designates a trusted person to make decisions about healthcare when the patient is unable to do so. Known as a "healthcare agent," this person steps in when a patient is mentally incapable, suffering from dementia, unable to communicate, or simply recovering from anesthesia. The healthcare agent can make timely decisions during situations that the Living Will does not cover or anticipate. The healthcare agent has the power to access medical records, visit the patient, choose medical facilities and personnel, and consent to or refuse medical treatment as long as the Living Will is not violated.

When selecting a healthcare agent, each parent should choose someone who inspires trust and knows them well. Parents usually select a spouse, friend, adult child, or a professional such as an attorney. Be aware that spouses are not always automatically considered to be Health Care Power of Attorney agents. Your parents must clarify this legal relationship with an *official document*. Mom and Dad each should pick one primary healthcare agent and one secondary healthcare agent. This secondary agent will assume the responsibilities if the primary agent cannot perform the job.

A Health Care Power of Attorney document must be created and signed by your parents while they are clearly mentally capable. This is a great reason to move forward on this document as soon as possible. The likelihood that your parents will become incapable increases as they age. The statistics are sobering. Alzheimer's is the most common form of dementia and the risk of developing the disease doubles every five years after age 65 and affects nearly 50 percent of people older than 85, according to the Alzheimer's Association.

If your parents become incapable of making medical decisions before they choose healthcare agents, then medical personnel will likely control the situation. You will be forced to obtain a designated guardianship in order to take charge of your parents' medical care. This can be a long and difficult process.

Health Care Power of Attorney documents differ from state to state. In many places, the state medical association has designed a standardized Health Care Power of Attorney form that will be recognized immediately by healthcare professionals in that state. Visit your state medical association's website to find out more information or discuss the form with your parents' attorneys.

HIPAA Forms

The Health Insurance Portability and Accountability Act of 1966 (HIPAA) Privacy Rule is one of the laws included in the Health Insurance Portability and Accountability Act of 1996, a set of laws passed by the United States Congress.

You should already be familiar with the forms required by the Privacy Rule. Every doctor's office asks you to fill out a HIPAA Privacy Authorization form on your first visit. This document is designed to prevent doctors from sharing medical information with people other than the patient.

Your parents must add your name to their HIPAA forms in order to give their doctors permission to talk with you. Make a list of your parents' healthcare providers and obtain the appropriate HIPAA forms. After your parents have added your name and signed the forms, return them to the healthcare providers.

2. Financial Documents

Here's something everyone should remember: **Talking about death won't kill you!** Discussing end-of-life issues with your parents can be difficult but the resulting peace of mind is priceless. Please take care of these essential documents before your parents need them.

The two most important *financial* documents for your parents are the Last Will and Testament and the Financial Power of Attorney. Depending on your parents' financial circumstances, they may want to consider a third financial document known as a Trust.

Legal matters can be confusing. With your parents, seek the guidance of an attorney and financial planner. Elder law attorneys (www.naela.org), healthcare professionals, and organizations specializing in eldercare issues can be particularly helpful with these difficult decisions. For more information, check out long-term-care ombudsman programs, community medical societies, medical centers, senior programs, and departments on aging at the local, state and national levels.

Last Will and Testament

A Will is a legal document designed to disperse a person's assets in an orderly way after death. This document allows Mom and Dad to leave legally binding instructions for distributing their assets after they pass away. Wills also enable your parents to select their own executors, the people responsible for managing the estate and dispersing the property, cash, stocks, and so forth.

When a person dies without a Will, each state has a set of laws that act like a default Will. In this case, state law dictates how the assets will be distributed, and the court selects and appoints an administrator to supervise this process. Shockingly, 55 percent of Americans do NOT have this essential legal document, according to Martindale Hubbell.

Both your mother and father should have Will. If they don't, *now* is the time to convince your parents to get to the attorney's office. Encourage them to be precise in their Wills. After Mom and Dad pass away, there will be less friction between family members if your parents have left behind detailed instructions. Many people get very specific in their Wills. If your mother wishes, she can leave her silver tea set and antique hutch to Aunt Bessie, the wide-screen television to her grandson, and her annoying Siamese cat . . . to you.

Mom and Dad each need to name an executor in their Wills. The time-consuming job of executor includes dealing with assets and debts, and communicating with beneficiaries and insurance companies. Ideally, an executor is trustworthy, responsible, and competent in money matters. Encourage your parents to ponder this decision. Sometimes a family member is the best choice. Other times, choosing an executor who is *not* a beneficiary may reduce friction and prevent conflicts of interest. Each parent should also name a successor executor, in case the first executor is unable to do the job.

Wills need to be updated at least every five years, especially if there has been a change in marital status, a death or birth that affects the Will, significant financial changes, a geographical move, or a reduction in Mom or Dad's physical or mental capabilities. If your parents tell you, "Oh, we took care of our Wills years ago," then you need to make an appointment with an attorney to review the documents. Unless Mom and Dad have created their Wills recently, the documents may be outdated or invalid because your parents' circumstances have changed. This is particularly important if your parents' Wills are more than five years old or were produced in another state.

Make sure their Wills are signed, dated, witnessed, and filed in a safe place.

Financial Power of Attorney

When illness, surgery, dementia, or another condition renders your parent unable to handle financial matters, a Financial Power of Attorney is invaluable. This legal document gives a particular person (a spouse, relative, or other trusted individual) the power to make financial decisions for your parent when Mom or Dad is unable to do so. This person is known as the "agent" and is permitted to manage everything from personal finance tasks, such as paying bills and depositing checks, to business and investment decisions.

If your parents are unable to handle their finances and they haven't selected agents, problems quickly pile up. For example, mortgage and utility payments are missed, insurance premiums and medical bills go unpaid, and issues arise with credit card debt and your parents' credit ratings. If Mom or Dad owns a business, the effects can be especially devastating. Like the Health Care Power of Attorney, the Financial Power of Attorney is designed to allow a responsible person to make timely decisions and act on matters not covered by other documents.

If your parents need help with their finances but haven't created a Financial Power of Attorney, then you must petition the courts to assign an agent. This legal process is long and expensive. Your parents can prevent this by naming their Financial Powers of Attorney *right now*.

Be aware that some financial institutions don't accept a general Power of Attorney and require their own individualized forms.

Trusts

A Trust can provide a tidy way for your parents to bundle their assets and transfer ownership directly to their beneficiaries without involving a Will or the complications of probate court. There are many types of Trusts. In general terms, a Trust allows a person to directly transfer ownership of assets after death. This means that the assets will not go through probate, which is the legal process designed to ensure that a Will is valid. The probate process can be time-consuming and expensive. Contrary to popular wisdom, however, a Trust may not reduce estate taxes or keep creditors from coming after the property.

Trusts are complex and not for amateurs. Avoid pushy salespeople, preprinted forms, and free seminars. Some of these may be scams. Instead, enlist the help of an experienced attorney specializing in probate or estate law to determine whether your parents will benefit from establishing a Trust.

Double-check Everything

Once the five critical documents are completed, double-check to make sure that all the papers are signed, witnessed, and notarized. Each state has specific requirements for signing of Wills, so make certain that your parents' documents meet these conditions. If the documents are not completed correctly, then they are not legally binding and will need to be redone.

Make copies of the five essential documents and distribute the appropriate papers to your parents, their physicians, your parents' hospital and/or care facility, the attorneys, agents designated in the documents, your siblings, and yourself.

Review the Documents Regularly

Mark your calendar with reminders to review these documents annually or as your parents' physical and mental capabilities change. Laws and regulations vary by state. If your parents move out of the state where they created the documents, then their documents may need to be modified or rewritten.

GLOSSARY

Advanced Directives. Legal documents enabling people to plan for a time when they will be unable to make their own decisions in medical and legal matters. Advance Directives include the Living Will, DNR, Financial Power of Attorney, and Health Care Power of Attorney.

Agent. A trusted person who has legal permission to conduct financial, medical, or legal affairs for another person. Also known as *Proxy*.

Assets. Everything of monetary value that a person possesses, including investments, life insurance, real estate, stocks, cash, cars, and other personal property.

Beneficiary. The person, organization, or entity that inherits assets from the estate of a deceased person.

DNR. An advanced directive for paramedics and other medical professionals instructing them not to perform CPR (cardiopulmonary resuscitation) when a patient's heart or lungs have stopped working.

Estate. All assets owned at the time of death.

Executor. The person given responsibility for carrying out the terms of a Will. The executor oversees the assets, pays debts, and distributes the estate to beneficiaries of the Will. This person is specifically named in the Will.

Financial Power of Attorney. Legal document that gives a person (the "agent") the power to act for another person (the "principal"). The agent has the authority to make decisions about the principal's property, finances, and business enterprises. Depending on the terms of the document, this power can be broad or limited. By setting up a Financial Power of Attorney, your parents can place a trusted person in charge of their finances when they are ill or disabled. [Note: The Financial Power of Attorney is not specifically designed for older people. It can be created at any point in the principal's life.]

Health Care Power of Attorney. A legal document that gives one person (the "healthcare agent") the power to make medical decisions for another person who is unable to express his or her wishes. This patient may be mentally incapable or unable to communicate due to illness, surgery, dementia, and so forth. The healthcare agent makes decisions about medical treatment in situations not covered by the patient's Living Will. Also known as *Health Care Proxy, Durable Power of Attorney for Health Care, Medical Power of Attorney, Designation*

98

of Surrogate, or *Patient Advocate Designation.* [Note: The Health Care Power of Attorney is not specifically designed for older patients. It can be established at any point in a patient's life, even in the case of temporary medical conditions.]

HIPAA. Also known as the Health Insurance Portability and Accountability Act of 1996 (HIPAA). Enacted by the United States Congress, this Act includes the HIPAA Privacy Rule, a law designed to keep medical information private and protected. Under this law, if your parents want you to have access to their medical information, then they must name you on the HIPAA Privacy Authorization forms on file with their medical professionals and facilities.

Last Will and Testament. A legal document detailing how a person wants his or her assets to be distributed after death. If your parents do not have Wills, they will have no control over their assets after death. Instead, the probate court will make the decisions about the estate.

Living Will. A legal document that clarifies the patient's wishes regarding medical intervention at the end of life. Once a person can no longer communicate his or her wishes, family members and medical professionals use the Living Will to guide their actions. Living Wills only deal with end-of-life decisions, so your parent also needs to select a Health Care Power of Attorney agent who will have the authority to make decisions on other medical issues. Also known as: *Directive to Physicians, Health Care Declaration, Health Care Directive,* or *Medical Directive.*

Notarized/Witnessed. Two ways to certify that a signature on a legal document is authentic and not a forgery. A document is *notarized* when it is stamped and signed by a notary public, who is an individual with the authority to authenticate the signatures on contracts and other documents. A document is *witnessed* when the signing of the document is observed by an uninvolved person who then adds their own signature as proof.

Ombudsman. An independent advocate. In the probate court, an ombudsman can help resolve problems and complaints, answer questions, and make recommendations to the court.

Probate. The legal process designed to ensure that a Will is valid. The probate court is the state court in charge of reviewing Wills and overseeing the transfers of assets after death. The probate court appoints either an executor (as named in the Will) or an administrator (if there is no Will). The executor or administrator is responsible for taking inventory and appraising the assets, paying debts, and distributing the estate to beneficiaries of the Will.

Trust. A legal arrangement that allows a person to control the distribution of his or her assets after death. Trusts can enable a person to directly transfer ownership of assets after death and avoid probate court. A Trust is created by the original owner of the assets (the "trustor") and managed by a person known as the "trustee". The assets will eventually become the property of another person or entity (the "beneficiary"). Trusts can be designed to continue after the trustor's death or to transfer the property directly to the beneficiary upon the trustor's death. [Note: A Living Trust is a revocable trust established during the lifetime of the trust's creator. The terms of this Trust can be changed at any time before death.]

Trustee. The administrator of a trust. This person or entity manages the trust's assets.

Trustor. The original owner of a trust's assets and the creator of the trust. Also known as *Grantor* or *Creator*.

Brendan

By Jim Berg

He stepped outside into cold air and moved away from the lights to a dark corner. The wind bit at his face. Orion's Belt was crystal clear in a dark sky, and he stared at it, trying to picture the rest of the constellation, the club and shield, trying to remember the name of the stars. He bent down and scooped up snow in his bare hands. The cold demanded his immediate attention and everything else slipped away.

Stepping back inside, he walked through the lobby and past the gift shop. As he entered the long hallway between the cafeteria and the ER, the florescent lights began to flicker, casting shadows all around him. He hated that hallway, the sterile white walls, the static air, the way it felt like he was walking endlessly uphill. And now the crackling electric bursts and the shadows.

He knew they were waiting for him in the little conference room off the ER, but he stopped at the fish tank. He rolled his head and lifted his shoulders; he took a deep breath and exhaled slowly. A tiny orange fish, built like a little scoop of ice cream, stared out at him with black curious eyes, its diaphanous fins and tail fluttering like streamers in a parade. Fish with black dots and blue strips and yellow lines darted behind the glass—an Impressionist painting given life and moving through the water the before him—but the tiny orange fish watched him with a fixed, inquisitive intensity, with little bubbles escaping his mouth and rising to the surface. Brendan poked the glass with a finger, and the funny little orange fish swam away.

At the conference room, Brendan opened the door and entered without a word, sitting on a small couch next to his sister, who took his hand, locking her fingers with his. He glanced at his brother, who had spent the last two nights at the hospital, and forced a small, tight, "We'll make it through this" smile on his face. His brother nodded warmly, but his eyes were red from exhaustion, his foot tapping like a metronome on the carpeting.

They waited quietly until the surgeon arrived a short time later. "You guys have been through a lot this last week," he said, wrapping both arms over a clipboard and pressing it to his chest. "So I'm not going to sugarcoat it. His chances are slim." The surgeon pushed his glasses up off his nose with a single finger. "And if he survives, his quality of life will be greatly diminished."

He glanced through the room at each of them, his chest rising as he took a breath, then sinking as he exhaled. "Did he fill out a Living Will? Or give one of you power of health care proxy?"

My sister spoke softly, "No."

"Then you'll need to decide as a family how heroic you want us to be in our efforts."

Silence.

"I'll be back in five or ten minutes."

Brendan felt his sister's grip tighten, a single nail biting into one of his knuckles; he saw his brother sinking back into the chair alongside of them. And he imagined the wind against his face, cold and raw, the snow numbing his hands.

Please Sit Down and Fill Out This Form—
Be a Great Advocate in a Medical Setting

- **Prepare in advance for medical appointments and hospital visits**
- **Be an effective caregiver in medical settings**
- **Ask the right questions in the doctor's office, emergency room, and hospital**

Once upon a time, my 82-year-old mother had a 10:30 a.m. appointment with her internist. I carefully marked out two hours in my calendar book, wrote the appointment down on Mom's big kitchen calendar, and called her the day before to remind her. I thought that I had done everything possible to make the morning go smoothly. Here's what happened:

9:45 a.m. *Leave work and head to Mom's apartment.*

10:00 a.m. *Open front door. Mom is sitting on couch in nightgown. Bite tongue before I say something. Smile. Hustle Mom into the bathroom. Tell her to brush her teeth.*

10:05 a.m. *Grab pants and blouse from the closet. Dig through the sock drawer to find a matching pair. Search for shoes under the bed.*

10:10 a.m. *Return to bathroom. Mom is still brushing her teeth.*

10:11 a.m. *My acid reflux kicks in.*

10:12 a.m. *Help Mom get dressed. Notice that she's having some trouble with her balance. Help Mom out to the car, walking slowly.*

10:25 a.m. *Drive to the doctor's office. Think nasty thoughts about the guy in front of me who drives five miles under the speed limit for the entire trip.*

10:40 a.m. *Pull car into the portico of the office building. Help Mom out. Sit her down on nearby bench. Jump back into the car.*

10:46 a.m. *Find a parking space in the garage. Sprint back to the bench where I left Mom. Bench is empty. Look around frantically. No sign of Mom anywhere.*

10:51 a.m. *Run into the internist's office, heart pounding. Hope to find her sitting there, waiting for me. Nope. I can't believe I've misplaced my own mother!*

10:53 a.m. *Two nurses help me scan the hallways, search bathrooms, and check other doctors' offices. Acid reflux shifts into high gear.*

11:00 a.m. *One of the nurses finds Mom in a women's bathroom on the second floor, in the third stall down.*

11:11 a.m. *Thank nurses profusely. Head back to doctor's office with Mom in tow.*

11:15 a.m. *Sink into chair in waiting room—sweaty, angry, relieved, and embarrassed. Quite sure that everyone in the waiting room thinks I'm a neglectful daughter. Now 45 minutes late.*

11:20 a.m. *Fill out forms for Mom. Get hand cramp.*

11:35 a.m. *Ushered into exam room with Mom. No magazines available. Only thing to look at is a poster of the digestive system.*

11:45 a.m. *Mom's physician enters the room. Starts collecting her medical history. Mom lists her childhood illnesses and then starts talking about the appendectomy she had when she was 24 years old.*

11:55 a.m. *Ten minutes pass and Mom is still talking about her appendectomy. Now we know all about her house, her job, her appendicitis symptom, and the lunch they served her at the hospital in 1937.*

12:00 p.m. *Doctor examines Mom and asks about her medications. Mom can recall only two prescriptions and doesn't know the dosages. Mentally kick myself for not writing down her meds and an important question about her diabetes that I now can't remember.*

12:35 p.m. *Get back into car. (I* do not *leave Mom sitting on the bench. Fool me once . . . .)*

12:45 p.m. *Stop by pharmacy to pick up Mom's new prescription. She doesn't have her prescription card, so I pay the bill.*

1:10 p.m. *Arrive back at Mom's apartment. Fix her a sandwich and bowl of soup. Make sure she takes the new medication.*

2:00 p.m. *Return to work, hungry, tired, and angry. Also feel guilty for being angry because Mom didn't intentionally drain my entire supply of patience and antacids. Put my head down on my desk. Wonder if every appointment will be this awful, and how long I can keep doing this. . . .*

I made a lot of mistakes that day. In the days following that appointment, I realized that I had to find a better way to handle my parents' medical appointments. I also realized that Mom and Dad would be hospitalized at some point, and I wasn't ready to help them navigate emergency rooms and hospital stays either.

Over the next several years, I worked to improve my caregiving skills in medical situations. I invested time in preparing for doctors' appointments. When I was in the emergency room and hospital, I learned how to deal with doctors, nurses, and my parents. Most importantly, I opted for valet parking the next time I took Mom to a doctor appointment! My goal was to be the best possible advocate for Mom and Dad while still taking good care of myself.

I've put all my best, hard-earned advice about these things into this chapter for you, so that—with a small investment of time and energy—you will be better prepared to face these same challenges with your parents. Start now and you'll soon be ready to walk into the physician's office fully prepared. You will also be able to manage emergency rooms and hospitals with less stress and better results.

Your #1 Survival Tool: "The Competent Caregiver Binder"

I know, *"The Competent Caregiver Binder"* sounds a bit silly, but preparing and carrying this binder with you will immediately give you credibility with any medical professional. When I was faced with juggling all of the medical information, forms, and appointments for both my father and mother, I devised this system to keep everything organized and portable.

Making your own *Competent Caregiver Binder* is the best way to prepare for a doctor appointment or hospital stay. You will have all the critical medical information right at your fingertips. Doctors will love you. Nurses will be impressed. Receptionists will actually smile when they see you coming! Healthcare professionals will get accurate information about your parents, and you will get speedier service.

With one trip to the office supply store, you can pick up everything necessary for making your own *Binder*. Here's what you'll need:

- One sturdy, one-and-a-half-inch, three-ring binder. If you are caregiving for both parents, you will need two separate binders.
- Binder pockets for loose papers.
- Clear plastic sheet protectors for papers that you will need to view often, such as your parents' medical histories.

- Two zippered pouches that are large enough to hold insurance cards, prescription cards, and information about any medications that you may need to show to the physician. (Look for inserts that are designed for use in a three-ring binder.)
- A calendar where you can record all your parents' appointments.
- Loose-leaf paper or a small notebook for jotting down your questions and the doctors' answers.
- Several pens and pencils to slide into the zippered pouch.

Next, follow the next six Steps to assemble the contents of your *Competent Caregiver Binder*. Don't let this job slide until the last minute, because you're likely to forget something.

Binder Step 1: *Create a Handy Medical History*

Having a parent's medical history ready for the healthcare provider is incredibly valuable. If I had prepared a medical history before Mom's appointment, we would have saved at least 15 frustrating minutes in the exam room trying to move her past her report about her 1937 appendectomy. More important than saving time, though, having a complete medical history in hand could save your parent's life.

You will be asked again and again for this information, so be ready. Once you've compiled the medical history, slide it inside a plastic sheet protector in the *Binder*. Here are recommended contents to include:

- List your parents' current physicians and their contact information. Tuck a copy of this information in your wallet or purse, as well.
- List all the prescription medicines that your parent is currently taking. Be sure to include the dosages and frequencies of the medications.
- If the medicine cabinet is full of bottles and you aren't sure which medicines are currently prescribed, scoop up the medications, drop them into a grocery bag, and lug the bag to the doctor's office.
- List all over-the-counter medications (such as eye drops, pain relievers, and cold remedies) and supplements (such as vitamins and herbal remedies). Possible interactions are difficult to anticipate, so list everything.

- Write down the contact information for your parents' pharmacy, including any specialty pharmacies.
- List all allergies and allergic reactions.
- List vaccinations and dates, including pneumonia and flu shots, as well as vaccinations for shingles, hepatitis B, and tetanus/diphtheria. Make a note to ask the physician if any other vaccinations are recommended.
- List all previous surgeries and other important medical treatments, including the dates.
- Note implanted devices and artificial joints.
- Compile a family health history for your parents. This means gathering medical information about their parents and siblings, including significant illnesses and causes of death. To determine how my grandparents died, I actually obtained the medical records from their hospitals and examined the doctors' notes.

Binder Step 2: *Get Your Parents' HIPAA Forms in Order*

The Health Insurance Portability and Accountability Act of 1996 (HIPAA) is designed to keep medical information private and protected. This Act prevents physicians and nurses from sharing your parents' medical information with you unless your name is listed on your parents' HIPAA Privacy Authorization forms. Nearly all doctors have their own HIPAA forms and will provide their patients with copies of these forms. If possible, collect Mom's and Dad's HIPAA forms in advance and prepare them with your parents. You can also request the forms during an appointment. Some states require HIPAA forms to be notarized, so determine whether this is necessary. Place the HIPAA forms in a *Binder* pocket for easy access.

Binder Step 3: *Print Name and Address Labels*

Use your computer to print out your parents' contact information (name, address, phone, email, and so forth) on adhesive-backed address labels and place the labels into a pocket folder. Rather than fill out the same information again and again on your parents' forms, you can simply peel and stick the labels.

Binder Step 4: *Make a List of Questions*

How many times have you visited your own physician, left the office, and *then* remembered something very important that you wanted to ask? Keeping track of those questions is even harder when you're trying to supervise your parents' healthcare. Don't try to keep everything in your head. Record your questions in your *Binder*, either on paper or in the small notebook.

Before an appointment, also consider these questions and write down your responses:

- What is the reason for the visit? Be specific. Is this a medical, emotional, or mental issue?
- What are Mom or Dad's symptoms? How severe are they? How long has your parent been having these symptoms?
- What daily activities is your mother or father capable and incapable of doing, both mentally and physically? This information helps the doctor decide how to include Mom or Dad in the conversation and treatment, and figure out what accommodations need to be made at home.

Binder Step 5: *Collect Cards and Medications*

Depending on your parents' capabilities, they may want to carry their own health insurance and Medicare cards. In this case, copy the fronts and backs of the cards and carry those copies in your *Binder*. If losing or forgetting items is an issue, make an effort to keep these cards in one of the zippered pouches. Medications can be added to the pouch shortly before the visit. The contents of one pouch should include these items (originals or copies):

- Your parent's valid photo ID
- Health insurance card
- Prescription card
- Medicare card
- Any medications you want to ask questions about

Binder Step 6: *Keep Your Binder Handy*

Designate a special spot in your house for the *Competent Caregiver Binder* so that you can quickly grab it when you head out the door to your parent's doctor appointment or in case of a medical emergency requiring a hospital trip. Always put the *Binder* back in the same location. Tape an index card or business card with your telephone number and e-mail address to the inside of the front cover, in case the *Binder* is lost.

Your #2 Survival Tool: "The Capable Caregiver Carryall"

Yes, I know. This is another silly name that I made up. But this moniker is absolutely accurate. When you head off to the hospital to help care for your parent, you should plan on being there for hours. Sometimes the situation may require you to stay at the hospital for one or two days. My first few trips to the hospital with my parents left me stressed and exhausted.

Then I realized . . . how could I be a good caregiver when I wasn't taking care of myself?

After that, I began bringing a small travel-bag packed with items that kept me comfortable, nourished, and mentally alert. Having those supplies with me dramatically reduced my stress level, and I became a better advocate and a better listener.

You probably own most of your *Carryall's* contents already. I didn't need to buy anything. My *Carryall* always contained these supplies:

- Cell phone charger
- Good book and/or magazines
- MP3 player with ear buds
- Refillable water bottle or several bottles of water
- Toothbrush and toothpaste
- Travel pillow and a small fleece blanket
- Sweater or sweatshirt
- Nutrition bars or other nourishing, nonperishable food
- Any medications needed by my parents and/or myself
- *Competent Caregiver Binder*

Tailor your *Carryall* to your specific needs. Stock it with the items that comfort, entertain, and nourish you. Other possible additions include puzzle books, needlework, knitting, e-book reader, and your laptop computer or tablet and its power cord.

Many parents have special medical or personal needs. Stock the *Carryall* with items that will help keep your parent healthy and comfortable during a long wait. My mother had diabetes, so I always carried a bottle of glucose tablets for low blood sugar in my *Carryall*. Other caregivers may include items such as adult diapers, a sweater, warm socks, or nutrition drinks.

Dealing with Doctor Appointments

I can't promise that you will *never* have a disastrous doctor appointment, but these step-by-step tips should help make the experience easier for both you and your parents.

Appointments Step 1: *Scheduling the Appointment—Take Your Time*

Visiting the physician can be very time-consuming. Be considerate of yourself and your parents when you schedule appointments. Leave yourself extra time to arrive, since Mom or Dad may be moving slowly, and be prepared to wait. If you over-schedule or don't allow extra time for unexpected circumstances, you'll be stressed out before you even walk into the doctor's office.

When I first started taking Mom to her doctors' appointments, I arranged everything based on my schedule and my fast-paced life. Without realizing it, I set Mom up to fail because I was thinking in terms of "Barbara-time." Instead, I needed to see the world in "Mom-time." Mom lived from minute to minute and had no sense of urgency.

Appointments Step 2: *Preparing for the Appointment—Get Out Your Binder*

Create or update your parent's *Competent Caregiver Binder* with recent information and medications. In case of delays, be ready to entertain yourself and your parent in the waiting room. Bring something for both of you to do: magazines, knitting, crossword puzzles, Sudoku, and so forth.

Appointments Step 3: *During the Appointment—Don't Be Shy*

During a trip to the physician, **asking questions is your most important job**. Doctors are storehouses of information. Take advantage of this by asking questions and writing down the answers in your *Binder*. To give you an idea of some useful things to ask, I've included a section on questions at the end of this chapter.

Remember that there is no such thing as a stupid question. You are now an advocate for your parent and can ask about anything that involves them. Trust your instincts. If you are worried about something, there's probably a good reason, so speak up. And if you find out that your worry is unfounded, that information is comforting too. You win either way.

If the situation allows, write down the physician's answers to your questions in the notebook or pages of your *Binder* before you leave the appointment. This can be helpful in several ways. First, you don't have to trust your memory—it's all safely written down. Second, if your parent doesn't recall what the doctor said, showing them the doctor's words is often more persuasive than trying to convince them yourself. Your parents value the advice of trusted third parties, such as their doctors.

Some caregivers like to bring along a tape recorder, so they can listen to the answers afterwards and make notes in the *Binder*, or replay the physician's advice for other family members. A recording also comes in handy if your parent starts to insist, "The doctor never said that." Many cell phones include audio- and video-recording features that may be useful.

If you discover that one of your parents' physicians is not helpful and won't answer your questions, consider switching to a new physician. One or both of your parents may feel attached to a particular physician, but if you find that their doctor hasn't kept up with recent medical advances or won't listen to you, seriously consider seeking help elsewhere.

Appointments Step 4: *Leaving the Appointment—Stop by the Front Desk*

Save yourself extra work by scheduling the follow-up appointment while you are still in the office. If the physician gave you a referral or recommended a particular test, make sure you get the necessary names, addresses, and telephone numbers. In most cases, the office staff can quickly provide contact information.

If you are visiting a specialist, double-check to ensure that the specialist sends a copy of all reports, labs, and procedures to your parent's primary care physician. Ask for your own copy for the *Binder*, as well.

At the Emergency Room (ER) or Hospital

Hospital Step 1: *Preparing for the Hospital—Grab Your Carryall and Binder*

Restock your *Capable Caregiver Carryall* before you leave for a hospital visit, and update your *Competent Caregiver Binder* too, if time allows. You may want to add the following additional information to the *Binder*:

- List of medicines and foods your parent consumed over the past three days
- Contact information for all the doctors treating your parent
- List of your parent's currently active medical problems
- Results of any recent tests, including EKGs and X-rays

Hospital Step 2: *Arriving at the ER—Find Your Parents*

If you did not bring your parent into the ER, determine where Mom or Dad is right now. The staff will take you to your parent. Depending on how many hours have passed, your parent will be in one of the following five situations:

- Still in the ER waiting to see a physician or receive test results
- Undergoing a medical test
- In the ER's Observation Unit (also known as a Continuing Care Unit), an area where patients can be held for up to 24 hours under observation, to determine whether hospitalization is necessary
- Transferred to a hospital room
- Released and sent back home

Hospital Step 3: *Spending Time in the ER—Be the Favorite Advocate*

This is a great time to befriend every healthcare worker in the ER. Treat the staff with respect, joke with them, and learn their names. Make personal connections with the people caring for your parent. Your attitude and personality can make Mom more than just "the diabetic lady in Bed 305."

Share your parent's medical history (located in your *Competent Caregiver Binder*) with the doctors in the ER. Provide them with any information they need.

Hospital Step 4: *Undergoing Tests in the ER and Hospital—Tag Along*

Tag along when your parent is wheeled off to take a test in the ER or hospital. Your presence will help calm Mom or Dad's anxieties during this confusing time. Also, be sure to double-check that the staff is giving the right test to the right patient.

Hospital Step 5: *Spending Time in the Hospital—Be Nice and Be Smart*

Remember how great you were with the staff in the Emergency Room? If your parent is admitted to the hospital, be nice and smart everywhere else there too. Greet people with a smile, learn their names, and bring doughnuts for the staff . . . you want to be memorable in a good way.

Treat the unit clerk especially well. The unit clerk is the clerical person working at the nursing station. The unit clerk is the gatekeeper of the unit and can be your best helpmate.

Every day, your mother or father will have at least three nurses—one for each eight-hour shift. Different physicians and interns will be popping in and out of the room. **Because of the lack of continuity of care, your presence at the hospital is essential**. You know more about your parent's medical conditions than anyone. You are the most likely person to spot a change in your parent's condition, as well as possible mistakes by the staff.

If Mom or Dad is in the Intensive Care Unit (ICU), the time you spend with your parent will be limited to certain hours and lengths of time. The number of visitors is also restricted. As a result, you may spend long periods in the waiting room, rather than sitting by Mom or Dad's bedside.

Hospital Step 6: *Dealing with Doctors in the Hospital—Talk Face-to-Face*

Physicians who work solely with hospitalized patients are called "hospitalists." They visit their patients at a particular time each day. This is known as "making rounds."

Talking with your parent's personal doctors and other hospitalists is a crucial part of caregiving. Try not to be intimidated. Your parent's physicians want you to be well-informed. Here are some important things to do:

- Keep track of your parent's doctors and hospitalists. List their names in your *Binder* and identify the role that they play in Mom or Dad's care.
- Find out when each hospitalist will be making rounds, so you can get firsthand answers to your questions when the doctors visit your parent's room.
- Share your parent's medical history (located in your *Binder*) with the doctors.
- When the doctors recommend tests and medications, ask questions. For more information on "Asking Questions," see the next section.
- Keep a separate notebook in your parent's hospital room. Jot down questions when they occur to you, so you will be ready to talk to whichever doctor walks in. You can also leave the notebook in your parent's room, so that siblings can also add their questions, and the family can share information. Do not leave your parent's *Binder* of information in the room—it contains sensitive, private information that should not be made available to strangers.
- Use the separate notebook to record information about your parent's tests: name of test, reason ordered, date administered, and results. You should transfer these to your parent's *Binder*, too.

Hospital Step 7: *Being the Best Caregiver—What to Do*

Remember that Mom or Dad may be scared or in pain. It's common for patients to be disoriented, weepy, or belligerent. Your parent might even hallucinate due to sickness, medications, or a reaction to anesthesia. Don't take any of these behaviors personally, even if you are receiving the brunt of your parent's confusion or anger.

You can set the tone in the room by being calm and reassuring. Look for ways to soothe your parent. Soft music, dimmer or brighter lighting, a backrub, a favorite television show, or a beloved movie can be effective. Look for any small adjustment that will reduce Mom or Dad's anxiety.

Your presence can be a source of solace to your parent as well. Do your best to be positive with your mother or father. Smile and talk about the grandchildren or reminisce about the past. Any subject that is comforting can be very helpful.

Give yourself breaks. This is very important. The best times to leave your parent are when Mom or Dad is sleeping or when another caregiver arrives to sit with your parent. When friends and family ask how they can help, encourage them to visit the hospital to provide you with a respite.

Be careful to avoid leaving during rounds, however, or when you expect a physician to stop by your parent's room. If you do have to leave to go to work or to care for your family, and there is no relative or family friend to step in for you at the hospital, consider hiring a companion or aide to stay with Mom or Dad while you are away.

Hospital Step 8: *Being the Best Advocate—What NOT to Do*

All of the following behaviors are unhelpful and may interfere with your parent's care:

- Arguing with your siblings or other relatives
- Hanging around the nursing station or congregating in the hall
- Making demands instead of requests
- Being noisy or disruptive inside or outside the room
- Acting as though you or your loved one is superior to any other patient, healthcare provider, or staff member

Hospital Step 9: *Leaving the Hospital—Plan Ahead or Face the Consequences*

After your parent leaves the hospital, here are the six possible scenarios for where Mom or Dad can (or may need to) go:

- Home with no outside support required
- Home with the support of hired help and/or modifications to the house
- Your home, which may also require modifications
- Rehabilitation facility

- Assisted living facility
- Skilled-nursing facility

If you and your parents planned ahead and have already investigated their options for in-home healthcare, rehabilitation facilities, assisted living, and skilled nursing, making this transition will be much easier. If you haven't had the opportunity to explore these living situations, you need to start immediately.

The timing of your parent's discharge is unpredictable. You could have three days to get ready . . . or three hours. From the moment your parent enters the hospital, you need to be thinking about what will happen when Mom or Dad leaves. Ask the doctors about the anticipated length of your parent's stay. Get the discharge details as soon as possible so you can begin preparing for the next phase after hospitalization.

Frequently, a designated social worker or clinical nurse is assigned to Mom or Dad at the time you parent is admitted to the hospital. This person monitors your parent's progress through the hospital stay and can assist you with post-discharge planning. These staff members are already knowledgeable about the facilities and services available to your parent, so use them as a resource.

Keep asking questions until you understand the next step in your mother or father's treatment and care. Useful questions include the following:

- Is my parent being discharged to home or to a rehabilitation facility?
- If able to return home, will my parent need skilled or unskilled assistance? What kind of assistance and for how long?
- If able to return home, will my parent need special medical equipment or in-home care?
- If going to a rehab facility, what are our choices?
- If going to a rehab facility, which facility would suit my parent best? Why?
- Which expenses will be covered by Medicare and/or Medicaid?
- If my parent has a long-term healthcare policy, what will the policy cover?

In cases where the hospital does not provide support with post-discharge planning, you may need to make the plans yourself. If Dad needs a rehabilitation facility, then ask friends, family, and his personal physician for recommendations. If Mom needs in-home care for several weeks, then phone reputable home-healthcare agencies, select one, and schedule the necessary help. If your parent will be moving in with you, then start preparing your home and family.

Asking Questions

A big part of your job as caregiver is asking questions and understanding the answers. Many people find doctors intimidating. The best way to get over that feeling is to talk to your parents' physicians, ask questions, and learn more. Knowledge will make you feel more confident. Some caregivers worry about appearing disrespectful if they ask questions. This is not the case. When you ask questions, you are not challenging a physician's authority. You are trying to be a great advocate for your parent. By remaining calm and paying attention to the doctor's answer, you are being respectful in the best possible way.

Remember that if you can't understand the physician's answer, your Mom and Dad certainly won't comprehend it either. In fact, they may be depending on you to turn around and translate for them after the doctor leaves. If you don't get an answer from the doctor that makes sense to you, keep asking. If you are still confused after speaking to the physician, talk to the nurse assigned to your parent. A nurse may be able to phrase the information in a clearer way. You can also call your parent's primary care physician. With patience and persistence, you will get a satisfactory answer.

Medications

Medications save lives. Many older people are now easily treated for conditions that would have been deadly years ago. But the more medications that someone requires, the more complicated things become.

Side effects from medications can look like symptoms of another ailment. Many medications interact with other medications, certain foods, vitamins, antacids, and so forth. Many drugs can be crushed and safely added to pudding or applesauce, but others, such as some extended-release medications, can be very dangerous if crushed and consumed. Others may make the food unpalatable.

Asking questions will help ensure the effectiveness and safety of your parents' medications. Some important questions to ask about medications include these:

- What is the name of the medication? Does it have any other names?
- Why is my parent taking this medication?
- What is the prescribed dosage?
- How often should my parent take this medication?
- Should this medication be taken at a certain time of the day?
- What are the instructions for taking the medication? With food, with water, on an empty stomach? Should you avoid lying down after taking it?
- What are the possible side effects?
- What are the possible interactions with your parent's other medications? With certain foods and liquids?
- What should we do if a dose is missed?
- Does this medication come in a generic version?
- Does this medication come in a liquid or other form that may be easier to take?
- Can this medication be crushed up or dissolved to make taking it easier?
- Do you have samples of this medication? If available, a sample will allow your parent to judge effectiveness and potential side effects before purchasing a 30- to 90-day supply.

Treatments

If your parent has a medical problem, the doctor may prescribe treatment. This can be as simple as wearing orthotics to address foot pain or as complicated as undergoing a chemotherapy regimen for pancreatic cancer. Educate yourself about the proposed treatment by asking questions such as these:

- What is the procedure for this treatment?
- What are the risks of this treatment?
- Are the results going to be worth the risk to my parent?
- Does this condition require aggressive treatment?
- What are the other possible treatments for this condition?
- Do people often get a second opinion in these circumstances?
- Is it time to start discussing hospice?

119

Tests

Even if your parents are healthy, they can expect to undergo tests. In almost all cases, testing is a necessary and valuable part of medical care. For physically fragile parents, however, determine whether the testing is worth the risks.

At one point my mother's cardiologist wanted to perform an invasive diagnostic test. "What would we do with the results?" I asked. He told me that the test is used to determine whether a patient needs open heart surgery. But my 90-year-old mother had diabetes and other complicating factors. The cardiologist admitted that, no matter what the test results, he would probably advise against surgery. "Then let's just skip the test," I told him.

Mom's physician was doing his job by attempting to provide us with information about all her medical options. Yet, by asking the right questions, I saved my mother from physical and mental stress as well as unnecessary discomfort, costs, and risk.

When a doctor advises a test, always ask the following questions:

- Is this a necessary test or an optional test?
- What is the procedure for this test?
- What are the risks? Do the benefits outweigh the risks?
- Are there side effects? How long will my parent experience these effects?
- How long will the test take?
- When will the results be available?
- What is the expense?
- Will the test be covered by the third-party payer?
- Depending on the test results, what action will be taken next?

Caregiving for a sick parent is the most exhausting and complicated part of a caregiver's job. Advocating for your mother and father in the examination room and hospital room requires you to be considerate, smart, and prepared—even though you may be feeling anxious, confused, and frustrated. This is really hard work, but you will get through this. With the right preparation and information, I know that you can do a great job.

My last, most important piece of advice? Please, never get so stressed out that you leave your Mom sitting alone on a bench while you park the car. It's a really bad idea.

Sitting at his Bedside

By Jim Berg

I sit in the darkness, staring at my father in the hospital bed before me. How did this happen? I wonder. The rock of my life so helpless now. So fragile. Lying there beneath a tangle of wire and drips like some damn experiment gone awry, lying there with little beeps and burps on a wall of monitors to convince us that he is indeed alive even while he remains as silent and still as a dead man.

I hold his hand and he squeezes lightly in return; I smile at the monitor on his finger, blinking red in the darkness. My sister joked that he looked just like E.T.—all shriveled and pale and cute with a big red flashing finger.

His grip tightens suddenly, stronger than it's been these last days, and he wakes, agitated, fumbling with the oxygen mask over his nose and mouth.

"Dad," I ask, "do you want me to loosen the mask? Is it too tight?"

He doesn't seem to notice I'm there. He struggles with the mask, his breaths short and punctuated.

"Dad," I say louder, and he looks at me with dreamy eyes (the morphine); I lean closer and put my hand to my face to mimic the oxygen mask. "Is the mask too tight?" I ask, pronouncing the words slowly and clearly. "Do you want me to loosen it?"

Recognizing me, he relaxes. He lifts a hand weakly to my face and scratches my nose, gazing at me with a soft smile on his face. I suppose it doesn't seem like much, my father scratching my nose, but I am overwhelmed by the unexpected clarity and tenderness. To me it is a defining moment: My father, in diapers and barely alive, more concerned with my well-being than his own.

Too Much Stuff!—

Make Mom and Dad's Home Safer or Downsize for a Move

- **Declutter your parents' home**
- **Downsize for a move**
- **Distribute Mom and Dad's belongings**

When I began caregiving for my parents, they had lived in the same house for 40 years. Mom and Dad rarely threw anything away, so they had four decades of accumulated possessions crammed into every nook and cranny. To avoid misplacing her purse and important papers in the mess, my mother kept them on the stovetop. She also hid dollar bills inside the oven. "This way, I always know where those things are!" she told me, proud of her own cleverness. I had a different reaction. I asked her to use the microwave instead and then I pulled the knobs off the stove and took them home with me. Mom had become very forgetful. I felt certain that she would set the kitchen on fire next time she tried to use an oven littered with dollar bills.

When I looked around their home, I saw disaster lurking everywhere. I imagined Dad tripping over a stack of unread newspapers and breaking his hip. I could see Mom trapped in her bedroom during a fire as the flames ripped through the 20 packages of toilet paper she had stored beneath the bed. The firefighters, forced to stumble through a maze of couches and tables and chairs, would never reach her in time.

My parents found the clutter distracting. They couldn't locate objects that they needed. When I came over to their house to clean, the clutter got in my way. Just looking at all that stuff made me feel tired and stressed. After a few months of this, I desperately wanted to help them declutter and make life easier for all of us, but my parents refused to get rid of *anything*.

Eventually, when Mom and Dad needed to move into an apartment in a retirement community, I had the opportunity to declutter and downsize. But as I began to sift through the house, I had a harsh realization. Most of my parents' belongings had started out as precious possessions. Yet, as Mom and Dad accumulated more and more items, these possessions had turned into clutter. By the time I stepped in to clean up, I saw most of their belongings as junk. And I guessed that if I tried to give my parents' stuff to my kids, they would consider most of it no more than *trash!*

I knew that my "minimalist" children would not be interested in the china figurines lining the bookcase shelves. Or my mother's carefully smoothed collection of used holiday paper. Or my father's 30 consecutive years of *National Geographic* magazines piled high in the basement. And I was very sure that *no one* would want the box of pencil stubs helpfully labeled, "TOO SMALL TO USE."

My parents did own lovely heirlooms and furniture that their family members would be honored to receive. However, most of the items cluttering up the rooms and filling the basement needed to be donated, recycled, or thrown away. And now I had to deal with this huge job, in addition to the stress of moving my parents.

Be a smart caregiver. Help your parents declutter and downsize *now*. You won't regret it.

Six Great Reasons to Declutter and Downsize

Most people use only *one-fifth* of their possessions regularly. My parents didn't need most of their belongings. Already confused and forgetful, Mom and Dad frequently misplaced items amid the clutter. The quantity of furniture and stacks of magazines and newspapers made their home unsafe. When the time came for me to empty out the house, I spent a tremendous amount of time and energy downsizing and cleaning. All this unnecessary stuff complicated everyone's lives.

Here are six excellent reasons why it is worth the time and effort to declutter and downsize your parents' belongings:

Reason 1: Prevent injuries. A pile of magazines, a lumpy throw rug, or a pair of shoes . . . any of these items can send a parent sprawling, especially if eyesight or mobility is impaired.

124

According to the American Academy of Family Physicians, falls cause more than 90 percent of hip fractures and 70 percent of accidental deaths in people who are 75 and older.

Reason 2: Improve fire safety. Paper-based clutter—letters, files, coupons, magazines, books—ignites very quickly. Clothing and furniture also burn rapidly. In a cluttered home, fire spreads more quickly because objects sit in close proximity to each other. Rooms crowded with furniture can slow or prevent escape and rescue, especially under dark or smoky conditions.

Reason 3: Improve access and mobility. Clutter and excess furniture create additional challenges when Mom or Dad has balance or gait issues. If your parents have trouble walking, then a clutter-free floor is a necessity.

Reason 4: Reduce your parents' confusion. Many parents struggle with dementia, confusion, and memory issues. Clutter aggravates these conditions, adding to their distress and making your job as caregiver more difficult. When I began caregiving for my parents, I noticed that my mother always wore the same two outfits, almost like a uniform. I quickly realized that her closet, jammed with years of clothing, overwhelmed her. So I hauled everything out and put back only ten tops and ten bottoms. With fewer clothing options, she actually had an easier time choosing her outfits.

Reason 5: Eliminate unnecessary work for yourself. Clutter makes more work for the caregiver—you've got to clean it and move it from place to place. You waste time rummaging through the mess to find the items that you need. Extra furniture means more dusting, more cleaning, and more surfaces that collect clutter. Just looking at all that stuff is tiring! Clutter is an energy vampire, sucking away your strength and giving back nothing in return. If your parents still clean their home themselves, expect them to be pleasantly surprised once they find out that less clutter means less work for them.

Reason 6: Save time and money in the future. By decluttering and downsizing *now*, you can locate and safeguard items of monetary and sentimental value, such as treasured family photos and your grandmother's pearl necklace. At the same time, you can get rid of possessions that are worn, outdated, useless, or unwanted. Then, when your parents need to move to a smaller home or a facility, half the job will already be done!

How to Work with Your Parents (Or Not)

If you can eliminate clutter while your parents are still living in their home, **DO IT!** This is an opportunity to involve your parents in the downsizing process while they are still capable. Downsizing in crisis—after injury, death, or due to an immediate move—will be much more stressful for all of you.

Try to recognize that this process is difficult for your parents, even under the best circumstances. They may procrastinate or otherwise passively resist your efforts. Some will be overwhelmed, particularly if they are struggling with forgetfulness, confusion, dementia, or emotional issues. Some will openly refuse to allow you to start decluttering, or to help once you've started.

Six weeks before my parents moved into an apartment, I decided that the three of us would declutter and downsize together. First, I lined up large cardboard boxes, all neatly labeled with the names of relatives and charities. I added more boxes for trash, recycling, and items destined for the new apartment.

In their living room, I began by holding up each item and asking Mom and Dad to tell me which box I should place it in. I prompted my parents with helpful questions such as, "Do you need this for the new place? Or should I donate to Family Services?" Each time, they would answer, "Put that one aside, Barbara. We'll decide later." Growing more and more frustrated, I finally announced, "I will touch everything only one time!" After that, we made some progress.

When I returned the next day, the boxes were empty! My parents had spent hours putting everything back. I wanted to cry. We had wasted an entire day. Right then, I realized that my decision to include them wasn't helping anyone.

So I changed my strategy. Starting over, I walked through the house, noting what Dad and Mom used on a daily basis. Based on this, I made a list of the essentials for their new place. We packed up only those necessary items and left everything else behind in their old home. After they settled into their new apartment, I returned to the house. With my mother and father gone, I could finally work efficiently. For me, decluttering and downsizing was much easier without them.

One of my closest friends helped her widowed 85-year-old mother move to a retirement community. Afterward, my friend told me, "My mother lived in a 3500-square-foot house. I can now say that I have handled every single thing in that big house. And Mom told me a story about each item. It took a *long* time to get her downsized."

If you are fortunate, your parents will assist you with this project. If they do, though, don't expect it to be a speedy job. For many people, memories are deeply attached to the things they've collected over the years. For some, their belongings are their diary! Your parents will need to say goodbye to their possessions as part of the process. There are ways to help them with this, which you'll find later in this chapter.

How to Declutter or Downsize

Whether you are decluttering your parents' home or downsizing in preparation for a move, the procedure is very similar. If decluttering, be ruthless about getting rid of unneeded possessions. If moving, first select the items and furniture that Mom and Dad need for their new home and then eliminate or give away everything else. Instead of treating the move as a crisis, view it as an opportunity to clean out the house and prepare your parents for life in a safer, healthier place.

The following steps may seem like a lot, but if you work through them one at a time, decluttering and downsizing will be go more quickly and be less emotional for everyone.

Step 1: Divide and conquer. List the possible destinations for Mom and Dad's possessions—to charity, to grandchildren, to the new apartment, to the dump, etc. Assign each destination to a large box or a separate spot in the house. Label each location or box with a sign to prevent confusion.

Step 2: Develop a system for sorting the items. Ask questions that help you and your parent determine what to do with the object: "When was this last used? Does it work? Are there people who need this more than you do?"

Step 3: Follow the "touch-it-only-once" rule. Once an item is picked up, it must go into one of the piles and stay there. If your parents insist on pondering the decision, then create a small pile of objects to revisit later. Don't let it turn into a *big* pile, though. Consider setting a limit, perhaps 20 items, to encourage them to be selective.

Step 4: Write down the stories. As you sort, ask your parents to point out the truly meaningful items and explain why they are significant. Jot down short stories about the pieces. Otherwise, these histories may be lost. Your parents may be more willing to let go of their things when they know that family members will appreciate what the items meant to Grandma or Granddad. Also, family members will like knowing the stories behind the objects they receive. Sometimes, background information can increase the value of an item, either sentimental or monetary.

I typed out my parents' stories about each major belonging, printed them, and simply taped the papers to the objects. This made it easy to send the object and story together when I dispersed my parents' possessions. You can also preserve the stories and photos digitally by recording your parents talking about each item.

Step 5: Use these stories to encourage your parents to make their Last Will and Testaments. This is an excellent time to discuss Wills with your parents. As your write down their stories, ask your parents to decide who should receive or inherit the object. Ask them if they have specified these wishes in their Wills. If your parents still need to write their Wills, convince them to do it now. *This is one of the most important documents they will ever have.* In fact, both you and your children should also have Wills. Seize this opportunity to make certain that all three generations of your family take this important step in planning for the future.

Step 6: Distinguish between the junk and the valuable items. I suggest hiring an appraiser to help you. An appraiser will know whether Mom's favorite wineglasses are expensive Waterford crystal or cheap goblets that she received for opening up a new checking account.

Step 7: Go on a treasure hunt. You may groan after you read this . . . but you should sort through EVERYTHING. You cannot just pick up armfuls of paper and toss them into the recycling bin. Look through files, paper piles, and drawers for hidden documents and cash. I found $500 under my parents' mattress! People hide valuables in the oddest places: shoes, drapery hems, flour canisters, books, ice cube trays, the undersides of drawers . . . even in the toilet tank. Look under rugs and behind paintings. You never know where something wonderful may be hidden.

One of my friends cleaned out her parents' house and sold it. Several weeks later, the new owners called her. "We found something we think you'll want," they told her. When she arrived, they handed over an old Folgers coffee can. She opened the lid to find a pile of rare coins. My friend was incredibly grateful that the new owners had poked around in the back of the bedroom closet—and that they were so honest!

Step 8: Hire professional help. If the job is too big or you are a long-distance caregiver, then you can hire specialists to declutter and downsize. Contact the National Association of Senior Move Managers (www.nasmm.org).

Step 9: Get the details on donations. Ask your parents about their favorite charities. Make calls to determine the type of items those charities accept. Some charities will refuse items such as furniture and electronics. Find out the easiest way to donate. Some charities pick up items at the house; others have drop-off centers.

Step 10: Learn about local recycling. Find out the rules for curbside recycling in your parents' neighborhood. You can also drop the materials at a recycling center. Know which substances are considered hazardous waste, such as oil-based paint, rat poison, and lawn chemicals, and drive them to the local drop-off facility.

Step 11: Find out the local trash pick-up rules. Some municipalities will pick up bulk trash for free. For large quantities of trash, consider renting a dumpster. If your parents live in a house, the convenience of having a dumpster in the driveway may be worth the cost of paying the waste removal company.

Step 12: Get rid of old prescription drugs safely. Your parents may have accumulated a lot of unused or expired medicine and supplements. *Do not flush medications down the toilet.* Some communities have drop-off programs. If your parents' area lacks this type of program, the Federal Drug Administration advises dumping medicines into a resealable plastic bag and mixing them with an inedible substance, such as coffee grounds or cat litter, to prevent anyone else from finding or using them. Then place the medications into your normal household bagged trash.

Step 13: Consider commercial shredding. Any documents containing account numbers, passwords, PINs, Social Security numbers, birth dates, and signatures must be shredded. You can shred the materials yourself or enlist the help of a paper shredding service. My friend hired a company that drove a truck to her house and speedily shredded the boxes of documents she took out to them in the driveway.

Step 14: Use every visit as an opportunity to declutter. Never leave your parents' home empty-handed. Offer to grab that stack of old magazines or the set of chipped root beer mugs. If your parents offer you something, *take it!* Even if you don't want it. Giving away possessions is much less traumatic for them than throwing the items in the trash. You may not want it, but don't offend them by saying that. Thank your parents, take the object home, and then give it away or toss it out yourself.

Remember that these are merely objects that have outlived their usefulness. They *do not* represent your parents. You are not being unloving by throwing these items away. Instead, you are relieving your parents of the burden of dealing with the clutter.

Staying Sane

After Mom and Dad moved into their apartment, I returned to their house to clean and prepare it for sale. When I first walked in the door, I almost turned around and ran back to my car. As I looked around the house, I felt panicky and overwhelmed. The overflowing closets. The piles of papers. The full-size basement where boxes and junk covered every inch of floor space. Emptying out and cleaning the 2200 square-foot ranch-style house felt like an impossible chore.

But my parents needed the money from the sale of the house. I felt responsible for getting the best possible price so that Mom and Dad would be financially secure for the rest of their lives. If my parents' money ran out, then my sister and I would need to support them. My parents were depending on me. So I started working.

I sorted, tossed, boxed, and recycled. I made hundreds of trips up and down the basement stairs and emptied out every closet, cabinet, and drawer. After scrubbing the walls and floors, I painted the rooms and ripped out the old carpeting. Under the dingy floor coverings, I found beautiful hardwood floors. Using select pieces of my parents' existing furniture and a few rented items, I staged the rooms to look inviting. I spruced up the landscaping and edged the lawn. The result? A lovely house that sold at a good price.

With all the stress and physical activity, I dropped 25 pounds over three months. But when I look back, I don't question the sacrifice. The results were worth the effort.

Decluttering and downsizing is a big job. Everyone feels overwhelmed at the beginning. Take small steps. Start with one room. Start with one closet. Start with only an hour a week. I can't tell you that decluttering or packing up your parents' home is easy, or that you'll be done in a few days. But you will get through this. Every minute you spend working on this job moves you closer to the finish line.

If you must declutter or downsize quickly, then ask for help. Involve your siblings and other relatives or hire a professional to work with you. Having extra hands makes the work go much faster.

During high-stress episodes, such as moving a parent or downsizing a home, caregivers need to take particularly good care of themselves. But, when your extra time and energy are consumed by caregiving, this is a *big* challenge. After several weeks of nonstop cleaning at my parents' house, I reminded myself that I needed to do something just for me.

So I started thinking. . . .

A massage? I didn't have the time. A pedicure? Not my favorite way to spend an hour. A dinner out? My husband worked late on most nights and the kids had sports practice. A big piece of chocolate cake? My stomach wasn't up to that. Finally, I settled on a hot cup of coffee from my favorite coffee house. That was my big treat. Seriously. Sounds ridiculous, huh? But it was quick and delicious. Just doing that one nice thing for myself that day *did* make me feel better. And I promised myself that I would do something truly nurturing when I finished up with Mom and Dad's home.

In the middle of trying to be kind to others, we need to be kind to ourselves, too. Get your sleep and your exercise, eat good meals, and take your vitamins. Do something nice for yourself every day, even if it's just grabbing a good cup of coffee at the drive-through.

Dispersing Mom & Dad's Stuff

As you declutter or downsize, you will find meaningful and valuable items that need to be dispersed among family members. This process can cause an *unbelievable* amount of conflict. Family relationships are very complex and a parent's illness or death places a lot of stress on siblings. People may act unethically or thoughtlessly. Old rivalries, such as who was the favorite child or who got the most help from Mom and Dad, spring to life again. Some parents may even distribute their possessions in a way to send one last nudge or insult.

I've heard so many stories of families who fought over their parents' possessions and now no longer speak. So, how do you avoid or diminish the conflict? The most important strategy is to talk openly with everyone in your immediate family.

Here is a step-by-step method to help prevent or reduce conflict over your parents' belongings:

131

Step 1: Encourage Mom and Dad to distribute some belongings now. This way, they can decide how to distribute their possessions *and* feel the satisfaction of seeing their loved ones enjoy the cherished belongings. When my mother and father needed to move into an apartment, I urged them to distribute items to family and friends so that everyone would have the opportunity to thank them for their thoughtfulness and generosity. "Get the hugs now!" I told them. **This approach also made it easier for Mom and Dad to let go of their things.**

Distributing some possessions now, while Mom and Dad are still with you, will also eliminate potential conflicts in the future. After your parents pass away, there will be fewer items to cause discord.

Step 2: Devise a system to disperse other belongings. A good system will allow each family member to receive something meaningful. For some families, this means distributing the items in terms of value; for others, the sentimental associations are more important.

Be aware that you can't predict which possessions will be especially significant to your parents and family members. A friend's grandmother insisted on giving her a little wooden cube designed to hold pencils. My friend was puzzled: "It was junky and old. It wasn't worth anything." Still, she accepted the cube and asked why it was so important. Her grandmother told her, "Because I remember it sitting on my grandpa's desk." Suddenly, that cube was no longer a piece of junk—it was a sentimental heirloom.

Step 3: Set a great example by communicating openly. Keep your siblings informed about Mom and Dad's plans for downsizing or moving. If you are in charge of dispersing your parents' possessions, try to keep the process as transparent as possible. I've got more tips for accomplishing this in the next section, "Making The List."

I met one man whose sister went into their parents' home after Mom and Dad died and took valuable jewelry and art without asking him. His response? He never said a thing. He didn't want to confront his sister. He worried about ruining their relationship. But stuffing away his anger had the same effect. Due to unspoken resentments and suspicions, these two siblings will never be close again. You don't want this to happen in your family.

Making "The List"

Many families need a transparent, practical system for distributing their parents' belongings. Your parents may need to downsize in order to move into an apartment or assisted living facility.

Or they may have passed away. If Mom and Dad have written down a list of possessions that they want to give their children, their recorded wishes usually simplify the distribution of their belongings. But what if they haven't done this?

I've found that the most sensible way to handle this type of situation is what I call *"The List."* This system works equally well with local and out-of-town family members.

The List is a written inventory of each item of monetary or sentimental value to be distributed. This inventory is sent from family member to family member. Each person chooses **one item** and then passes *The List* onto the next person. This orderly method of distribution allows each person to consider the choices without any pressure.

I came up with this formula after my parents passed away and I couldn't find any good advice on what to do. I wasn't sure if *The List* would work, so I was delighted when my family responded positively. Since then, I've seen other experts propose similar techniques, which tells me that this process works well for many people and helps strengthen families instead of tearing them apart.

The List involves a simple procedure with five steps:

Step 1: Hire an appraiser to identify and price valuable items. Knowing the actual monetary value of these things will help your family divide your parents' property fairly.

Step 2: Decide who will receive *The List*. In my case, my sister and I agreed that our four kids would be equal partners with us, so we had six family members involved. With extended and blended families, this step may pose a challenge. Consider what your parents would have liked and give weight to the concept of "keeping things in the family."

Step 3: Make a draft list of the belongings to be shared. This can be a tedious task and goes much faster if you have a helper. If you can, put dollar amounts next to items of monetary value. Share the draft of *The List* with family members and ask if you have overlooked any items that should be on it. You may have missed belongings that have sentimental value for a particular person.

Step 4: Randomly assign numbers to each recipient of *The List*. I numbered six pieces of paper and pulled them out of a tissue box.

Step 5: Send *The List* to each recipient by rotating through the number order. For example, family member Number One gets *The List* first, jots down a "1" next to the blue Oriental rug and then sends The List to Number Two, who puts a "2" next to the pool table and then passes it to Number Three, and so on. Once *The List* reaches the final recipient, it is returned to Number One and the process begins again, until all of the items have been claimed.

In my family, *The List* traveled by e-mail from house to house, all over the United States and Canada. Then something wonderful happened. None of us seemed to care anymore about the monetary value of the items. Instead, my family members made their choices based on sentimental value. One grandchild wanted Grandma's favorite rocking chair and another chose the old armchair that her cat loved to curl up on. Some of the really nice antiques went unclaimed! Only one item ended up with two ardent admirers—my son and my daughter. They had a brief discussion and agreed amicably to send the huge antique hutch to my daughter, who was settled in a house, with the understanding that she would enjoy it until her brother had a home with enough space for the hutch.

If your parents are moving to a smaller home or an assisted living facility, they may want to see how their children and grandchildren are enjoying their "living inheritance." So once everything is dispersed, ask for photos of your parents' possessions in their new locations. When I visited my kids, I made sure to snap pictures of my parents' former possessions in their new settings. This was very helpful later when Mom got confused and asked me who had "stolen" her quilts or what had happened to her marble-topped antique table. I showed her the photographs and explained that the grandchildren were enjoying her lovely gifts. This soothed her, as the items were no longer "lost," and made her feel generous and more connected to her grandkids. She particularly liked to hear how her great-grandson now sat in *her* old rocking chair every evening to hear his bedtime story.

A Warning about Storage Units

When your parents move into a smaller place, try to resist the temptation to rent a storage unit and pile everything inside. You may think that you don't have the time or energy or emotional strength to go through all that stuff, and a storage unit would be a fast and easy option. Once you fill up that compartment and pull down that door, though, you won't want to go back. People tell me, "We haven't walked back into our storage unit for ten years." Meanwhile, they are spending over a thousand dollars a year on 100 square feet of space, storing stuff that grows more dusty and dilapidated every day.

What About Your Clutter?

Downsizing my parents' house took weeks. They had never considered the fact that someone would eventually have to empty out their home. As I worked, I worried about leaving behind a house full of clutter and useless items for my children. The idea horrified me. I didn't want them thinking, *"Why did Mom and Dad leave all of this for us to do?"*

When I was cleaning out my parents' house, I returned home exhausted every night. Yet I was determined to clean out my own closets and clear off my counters. Actually, I was more than determined; I was totally obsessed. After dealing with my parents' clutter for hours and hours every day, I couldn't tolerate ANY messy closets or stray knickknacks or piles of paper. I wanted to throw anything resembling clutter into the trash—immediately!

My wonderful husband, on the other hand, didn't share my panic. Over the years, I've come to realize that Bob is both a pragmatic saver and a sentimental saver. Unfortunately, just about *everything* in the world falls into one of those two categories. You may have someone like this in your life. I've already told the kids that, whenever we move out, any messes they find still left in the house belong to their father!

Even so, I followed Bob's lead and calmed down. I promised to never throw out the treasured memorabilia on his desk or the stack of wood scraps in his basement workshop. But I also realized that I could reasonably set aside a few hours every week to declutter the rest of our house. I started by placing a trash bag in the middle of my closet. I vowed to fill up the bag each week and donate it. To my amazement, my husband pitched in. As the clutter slowly disappeared from my house, I felt lighter, as if a big weight had been lifted. And I discovered that decluttering had unexpected benefits, including these:

- I could find items more quickly and easily.
- Cleaning took less time because I had less "stuff".
- I felt less anxious because I was responsible for less stuff.
- I discovered "lost" items.
- I felt a wonderful sense of accomplishment.
- I set a great example for my kids.

Not too long ago, I spoke at a conference on estate law. After my speech, an attorney approached me and shared a story about cleaning out his elderly parents' house. As his family rummaged through the basement, they found a large box marked "Important Papers." His Mom or Dad had taken the trouble to box up some files, identify them as essential, and then cart them down to the basement and ignore them for years. Someone lifted up the dusty box and they all started laughing. Underneath was an even older box with the label, "VERY Important Papers."

Over the years, we accumulate so much stuff that we do not need.

Get rid of it!

Decluttering my house was one of the smartest things that I ever did. The average person spends 55 minutes a day looking for misplaced items, according to a study quoted by *Newsweek*. By getting rid of all my excess stuff, I gave myself the best gift of all—more time to spend with my friends and family.

When the weight of the world is on your shoulders

And you're lost as a child without a home

When the winds of change are blowing colder

Just remember, you're not alone

I'll be there for you, I'll be there for you

So if you ever feel that you're not enough

Or if the road you're on is gettin' too rough

And goin' it alone has got you givin' up, remember

I'll be there for you

When the rain in your heart is never ending

And the dark clouds are all that you can see

When the hole in your soul seems way past mending

Just remember, you've got me

I'll be there for you, I'll be there for you

So if you ever feel that you're not enough

Or if the road you're on is gettin' too rough

And goin' it alone has got you givin' up, remember

I'll be there for you

"I'll Be There For You"

By: Karen Taylor-Good & Ed Tossing

137

Time for a Change—
Help Mom and Dad Find the Best Place to Live

- *Assess your parents' current housing needs*
- *Help your parents make housing decisions now and for the future*
- *Learn about the housing options available to your parents*
- *Provide support for parents living in their own home*
- *Prepare parents for a move to long-term housing*

The last time I visited my dentist, the hygienist told me about her 88-year-old father. He lives alone in his house, more than two hours away. He needs a walker, can't get down the front steps safely, can't see or hear well, and has fallen numerous times. He is so fragile that his physician called her with a warning: "The next time your dad falls, he probably won't be able to get back up."

Yet her father refuses to move out of his home or stop driving. He turns down offers to move in with her or her brother, and insists that he "won't give any of his money" to an assisted living facility. She regrets not convincing her dad to leave the house four years ago, after her mother died. "He was physically okay, so we let him stay. But that's when we should have told him to make a decision to move in with one of us. Now, he's dug in his heels and won't move out."

This loyal daughter regularly makes the five-hour round trip to her father's house to care for him while juggling the needs of her own family and a full-time job. The stress is enormous and she doesn't know what to do. "It's amazing what I'm going through for a person who I love so much but who drives me crazy," she says. "No court or attorney can get him out of the house. Unfortunately, it will take a catastrophic event like a broken bone or a car accident."

Four years ago, my kind-hearted hygienist and her brother didn't want to push their grieving father out of his home. In the midst of a crisis, they made short-term plans and did nothing to change Dad's living arrangements. Now, four years later, the family is trapped in an impossible situation.

As your parents get older, short-term plans grow less and less useful. Planning for the future is the key to effective caregiving, especially when dealing with housing. Looking six months or a year down the road isn't enough. You need to think in terms of years . . . and maybe even decades. Caregiving for the elderly is a marathon, not a sprint.

Facing the Facts

In my experience, caregivers tend to choose short-term solutions for two reasons. Running from crisis to crisis, they put out the immediate fires, but feel too overwhelmed to work on fire prevention. In addition, caregivers often have so many conflicting emotions about their parents' future that they don't feel ready to deal with those challenges.

Ready or not, every caregiver *must* understand, accept, and act on these three undeniable facts: **Your parents *will* get older and less capable, they *will* have at least one health crisis, and they *will* die.** According to AARP, over two-thirds of people age 65 and older need long-term care at some point. The average length of care is three years, and approximately 20 percent of these seniors need five or more years of care. Based on these statistics, it is very probable that **your parents will *not* be capable of staying in their home for the rest of their lives.**

No one wants to admit that Mom and Dad will require more and more help in order to stay in their own home. No one wants to admit that their parents may eventually need long-term care—not you, Mom and Dad, or your siblings. I understand that. But once your family wraps their minds around these ideas, planning for the future gets easier.

Getting older is not a choice or a punishment. Having to move out of your home is not a failure. Asking for help and planning for the future takes strength and bravery.

With your help, your parents can gain a sense of control by planning ahead, *now*. Although Mom and Dad don't have any choice about getting older, they can make decisions about when they will move and where they will live. Making those active choices together now, well before your parents *have* to move, will take much of the anxiety out when that day does come.

Every Crisis Is an Opportunity for Change

Crises are a part of caregiving. Many people begin caregiving in the middle of crisis, just as I did. When this happens, caregivers are understandably overwhelmed by the sudden changes, the new demands, and their parents' uncertain future. Crises are frightening, stressful, and anxiety-provoking for caregivers. These feelings are completely normal. Very likely, Mom and Dad feel the same way.

So, crises are awful. Right?

Yes, they are, but I'm going to tell you something else: **Crises can be very useful**. They give you and your parents an invaluable opportunity to make changes. Most of us, especially as we get older, tend to avoid change. We fool ourselves into thinking that everything will remain the same for the rest of our lives. Sometimes we need a crisis to compel us to change our lives for the better.

Crises create chaos. During a state of chaos, people are more open to change. In the midst of a crisis, your parents' lives are like boats that have broken free of their moorings. This can be frightening and disorienting. Fortunately, a drifting boat can easily be turned in any direction. If someone steps up to steer the wheel, then the boat can quickly set off for a better and safer location. But if the boat remains adrift, it will end up on the rocks. And if the boat is refastened to the original mooring, the same problems will repeat themselves. Use a crisis as an opportunity to take the wheel and change your parents' situation for the better.

Crises also offer an opportunity to face new challenges and experiences. Even though most aging people resist change, humans at every age actually thrive when required to change and adapt. We wither when deprived of stimulation and socialization. Your parents are more resilient than you think. They are more resilient than *they* think, too. Big changes, such as moving to a new home, will force your parents to create new patterns, meet new people, and adjust to a new "normal." A new home means that your parents will need to work their minds and bodies in new ways, which can lead to a healthier, happier, and possibly longer life.

Know the Options

Nowadays, your parents have lots of housing choices. Each type of housing serves a certain segment of the senior population. Your parents' first decision is choosing between a private residence and a facility designed especially for seniors. The second half of this chapter explores housing in greater detail, but here is a simplified overview.

If you parents want to remain in a **private residence**, they have three main choices:

- Stay in their home, with modifications and assistance as needed.
- Move in with relatives, or invite relatives to move in with them.
- Move into a smaller place, with modifications and assistance as needed. This includes apartments, condos, co-housing, and active adult communities.

If your parents decide to move into a **facility designed especially for seniors**, their options include the following:

- An independent living community
- A continuing care retirement community, which offers a range of housing from independent living to skilled nursing
- An assisted living facility
- A skilled nursing facility
- A facility designed especially for patients with dementia.

Since the 1950s, the average American lifespan has increased by about ten years. Ten years! This huge demographic change has increased the demand for senior housing and created a market for innovative housing concepts that should continue to grow for at least a decade. As a result, I expect the number of housing options to expand as we move further into the 21st Century.

142

Should They Stay or Should They Go?

When trying to identify the most appropriate housing situation for Mom and Dad, assessing their current abilities is the first step in determining the best ways to help them stay safe, healthy, and happy.

I often remind my audiences that assessment checklists are crucial, because "You can't *manage* it if you can't *measure* it." Discussions about moving often become emotional. Doing an assessment gives you the facts you need to help keep the conversation on track. Clear information on a checklist is much more convincing than an opinion or a feeling, even when that opinion or feeling may be completely justified. The results of an assessment also provide a quick way to update siblings on your parents' status.

The **assessment guidelines** in **Chapter 2: Stop, Look, and Listen** will help you determine the types of assistance and living arrangements that will benefit Mom and Dad. A thorough assessment will give you a clear idea of your parents' statuses on the continuum between "completely independent" and "needing around-the-clock care."

A Changing Life for Mom and Dad

Needs assessment is an ongoing process. After the first assessment, continue to track your parents' statuses. Expect their needs and abilities to change over time.

These shifts can be divided into the three major stages of senior life: independent, challenged, and protected. Each stage demands a different level of caregiving and, oftentimes, a different type of housing. Your parents' needs may change *within* each stage as well. By conducting regular assessments, you will be able to track your parents as they advance through this continuum. Don't expect Mom and Dad to both hit the same stage at the same time. It's very likely that their physical and cognitive abilities will decline at different rates and they will face different challenges.

Stage A: *An Independent Life*

In Stage A, your parents are able to live an independent life. You will know this because your assessment will show that your parents can successfully perform all the basic acts of daily living, including feeding, bathing, and mobility, without assistance. (For a complete list of the basic acts of daily living, see **Chapter 2**.)

Here are **significant behaviors that show your parents are in Stage A** and can continue to live independently:

- Eat a healthy diet on a regular schedule.
- Monitor their own health and take their medications properly.
- Dress appropriately, shower regularly, and take care of their teeth and hair.
- Maintain the household by cleaning, doing laundry, going shopping, etc.
- Handle their finances successfully.
- Provide their own transportation and, if driving themselves, drive safely and competently.
- Behave with emotional stability and show high cognitive functioning.

Stage A housing options. Right now is a great time to downsize to a **condo, apartment, or smaller home**. Some parents may prefer to move into an **independent living community** if they want fewer household responsibilities and more social interaction. If they are in a **continuing care retirement community**, seniors may live in their own apartments during this phase.

Stage B: *A Challenged Life*

In Stage B, your assessment will show that your parents are struggling or failing to perform some important everyday tasks. Here are **crucial indicators that your parents have entered Stage B:**

- Unable to clean the house by themselves.
- Fail to pay the bills accurately and on time.
- Stop bathing and performing personal care adequately without help.
- Fail to prepare nutritious meals without assistance.
- Unable to monitor their own health and take medications on time without oversight (such as visits from a skilled nurse).
- Fail to seek out or obtain adequate social stimulation in their current living situation.

144

- Drive unsafely or refuse to use safe alternative transportation.
- Behave with diminished emotional, physical, or cognitive stability (that is, they have difficulties that make living at home unsafe or impractical).

Stage B housing options. Generally, this phase is the longest and most challenging for both parents and caregivers. As Mom's and Dad's needs change over time, they will require outside help in order to keep **living at home, with relatives**, or in an **independent living community**. If staying where they live now, their homes may need to be modified in order to provide a safer, more accessible environment.

For parents facing a significant number of challenges, an **assisted living facility** is often the best fit. In these facilities, every aspect of life has been tailored to suit this phase of life. People living in a **continuing care retirement community** (CCRC) may transition back and forth between the other levels of care available at their CCRC.

Stage C: *A Protected Life*

In Stage C, your assessment will show that your parents are highly unlikely to be able to live on their own and require significant daily care beyond what you and your family can provide. Here are **critical facts that show that your parents have entered Stage C:**

- Require around-the-clock caregiving due to mild dementia, decreased mobility, medical conditions, or other physical and cognitive challenges.
- Display moderate to severe dementia that requires special care and safety provisions.
- Need the daily attention and supervision of numerous skilled medical professionals.
- It becomes more cost-effective for them to move into an assisted living or skilled nursing facility, due to the level of in-home care needed.

Stage C housing options. At this stage, parents need the most attention and care. Living at home or with relatives may become impractical or impossible. **Assisted living facilities, skilled nursing facilities**, and **specially designed dementia facilities** provide moderate to high levels of day-to-day support and medical services.

If your parents are already in a **continuing care retirement community**, they can transfer to and from their CCRC's assisted living facility and skilled nursing facility during this stage, as needed. Be aware that a transition into a skilled nursing facility is not necessarily a parent's final move. In some cases, residents improve and can return to assisted living. Spouses requiring different levels of care may need to reside in separate areas of the CCRC. This worked out well for my parents. After my mother moved into the assisted living facility at their CCRC, my father remained in their apartment nearby and could easily visit her whenever he wished.

Sit Down and Talk: Three Tough Discussions

After you've done thorough assessments of your parents and their current housing, family members should meet to discuss the situation and consider the best plan for the future.

Discussion 1: *Planning for the Future*

If you, your parents, and your siblings work together, you can design a housing plan that meets Mom and Dad's needs, both in the present and the future. These conversations can be challenging, especially if your parents are feeling anxious or vulnerable. Review **Chapter 3: I Love You and I Want to Help You** and **Chapter 4: We're All in This Together** for helpful tips.

The assessment results provide a starting point for creating the your parents' housing plan. Using the objective information supplied by the assessments, examine your parents' current challenges and work with your family members to address the existing situation. From there, help your parents design a plan for the future.

Ask Mom and Dad how they envision the rest of their lives. Your parents will probably want to remain independent and in their own home for as long as possible. Remind them that, as their child, you want to keep them safe and healthy. Acknowledge that settling on a plan that satisfies everyone may be a big challenge.

Not everyone will want to talk about the future, especially when you begin discussing assisted living and skilled nursing facilities. But it is important for your parents to make these decisions in advance. Even if Mom and Dad are in excellent health right now, they may eventually need these facilities. As their caregiver, knowing your parents' preferences in advance is both helpful and reassuring.

Be direct and discuss specific questions, such as the following:

- What changes should we make to your home so that you can age in place safely?
- When you need more help with cooking, cleaning, and maintenance, what would you like to do?
- If you get sick, what nursing facility do you want to stay in?
- If you develop dementia, where is the best place for treatment?

Your parents may initially dodge some of these questions. They may not want to hear that they need to remodel their bathrooms, or hire in-home care, or move to a new residence. Even if Mom and Dad can live independently right now, they may not appreciate your asking them to plan for a future where they get sick or can no longer drive.

Be patient. These discussions are *necessary*. You are not being disrespectful by proposing these changes or asking these questions. On the contrary, you are being loving and caring and, in many cases, brave.

You are also being realistic. On average, Americans who reach age 65 can expect to live at least 18 more years. The transitional period between fully independent living and end of life can last ten years or more, which is longer than in previous generations. My grandfather was diagnosed with cancer and died within months. In contrast, my father developed Parkinson's-plus syndromes and declined slowly for eight years after moving into a continuing care retirement community. Initially, Dad lived in the independent living section of his CCRC with my mother. Gradually, though, he developed balance and stability issues, emotional difficulties, and dementia. Eventually, Dad transitioned into the skilled nursing facility of the CCRC. It was a long journey for all of us.

Discussion 2: *Making Plans, Not Promises*

At some point, your parents may ask you to make promises about the future. Here's a really important piece of advice: **Do not make any promises about housing**. *Especially* if Mom and Dad are pressuring you. Do *not* agree to take them into your home when they can no longer live

147

alone. Do *not* promise to visit the assisted living facility every day. Do *not* vow to never move them into a nursing home. You may have wonderful intentions, but **you cannot predict what will happen in the future**.

Their health and capabilities will change. Your family and your career may change. Events that happen in a few months or a few years may force you to break your promises. Even worse, trying to keep your promises may push you to the breaking point.

Make *plans* about housing, not promises. Having a plan will make everyone feel more secure and protect you from having to make crucial housing decisions during a crisis. In addition, when you find a facility that meets your criteria, you can place your parents' names on the waiting list. Your mother and father may not be ready to move yet, but placing them on the waiting list means that they have a plan for the future. Then, when Mom and Dad *do* need a more supportive living arrangement, they will be able to get into their top choice more quickly and easily.

Be smart. Instead of making promises about housing, make a promise that you can keep: **Promise to always be there for them**.

Discussion 3: *Coping with Your Parents' Fears*

If the assessment reveals that Mom and Dad need to make the move to a long-term care facility, they may experience a wide range of negative feelings. These reactions can interfere with their decision-making ability. Mom and Dad may yell, cry, give you the silent treatment, or refuse to move. Instead of arguing with them, try to determine the root of their feelings and fears, and then present solutions that will help reduce anxiety and dispel misinformation.

Here are some of the thoughts that may be running through your parents' minds, and solutions for how to deal with them:

- **Fear based on old stereotypes.** Your parents may believe that they only have two choices: living independently at home or trapped in a bed in a dilapidated nursing home. *Solution:* Review the second half of this chapter and educate them on the wide array of housing options for seniors.

- **Fear of the unknown**. Moving to a new place means adjusting to a completely foreign environment with new rules, new schedules, and new people. Moving isn't easy for anyone, and adapting to change gets tougher as you grow older.

  Solutions: Respectfully listen to your parents' fears and address them. Tour the new place without your parents and gather useful information for them. Show them photos. Before the move, visit the facility or community with your parents several times to take a tour, eat a meal, or attend an event.

- **Feeling overwhelmed**. Even under the best circumstances, moving involves a staggering number of decisions and a lot of chaos. Dealing with the situation is especially daunting for a parent who is already struggling with confusion and forgetfulness.

  Solutions: Declutter your parents' home and make decisions with them about the disposition of their belongings, early. If possible, pare down the number of decisions or divide them into smaller bundles. For instance, I made a scale model of my parents' new apartment to help us decide what furniture to take and where to place the pieces. Weeks before the move, we decided what items to bring and where we would put them. Moving in became much simpler because we had a plan that everyone agreed on.

  If the job is still too overwhelming or contentious, then consider hiring a Senior Move Manager who has been specially trained in downsizing and moving older adults.

- **Anger.** Fear and frustration often provokes anger. Your parents may take their anger out on you.

  Solutions: Address the underlying fears and concerns. Remain calm and set clear boundaries. If you need to walk away from the discussion and wait for another day, then do it.

- **Loss**. Many different types of loss accompany these kinds of moves. Mom and Dad may be saying goodbye to their independence, their longtime friendships, their comforting routines, and a home full of significant memories.

  Solutions: Visit their new home often. Connect your parents with an acquaintance who also lives in the same facility or community. Make sure your parents' apartment or room contains familiar furniture and objects. Invite Mom and Dad's friends to visit them and treat everyone to a meal. Call their house of worship and request a visit from a member of the staff or a volunteer. Encourage your parents to rediscover old hobbies or explore new interests through the activities offered at their new residence.

- **Fear of death**. For some parents, moving into a facility designed for older people can be seen as the beginning of the end.

  Solution: Tell them stories of other people whose lives improved after their move. Due to the great care of the nurses and a new social life, my mother blossomed in assisted living.

- **Fear of the new**. Once they move, Mom and Dad won't be insiders anymore—they won't know the routines, the residents, or the staff. They will be shopping at a new grocery store. Everything changes.

  Solution: Some facilities offer short-term stays. This allows your parents to test out a community or facility. You can plan their stay to coincide with a vacation or to give you a respite from caregiving. The visit will give them the opportunity to see the everyday pluses of moving to a new place—less cooking, fewer chores, and no maintenance jobs.

- **Financial worries**. Like anyone else, your parents will be concerned about having enough money to cover their expenses.

  Solutions: Discuss how budgeting will be simpler after moving, so finances won't be as confusing. Look at their financial situation over the next few decades, rather than the immediate future, to create a feeling of security. Pay with Medicare or long-term care insurance, if applicable. If not, ask siblings to share the expenses.

What If the Answer Is Still "No"?

Even if moving is their best choice, your parents may still refuse to leave their home. As mentally competent adults, they have the right to say "No." Remember that you can't control them—you can only control how *you* deal with the situation. See **Chapter 3** for more advice on strategies for communicating effectively with your parents.

Housing Options for Mom and Dad

There are two basic choices when working with your parents and family to choose Mom and Dad's current and future residences. **Housing Option 1** is for your parents to remain in a private residence, such as their current home or another, more age-appropriate one. This may involve making changes to the residence, as well as providing in-home assistance from family members or skilled professionals. **Housing Option 2** moves your parents, either now or in the future, into a residence specifically designed for seniors, where some or most of the support services provided are performed by professionals.

Option 1: *Living in a Private Residence*

If you parents want to remain in a private residence, they have three choices:

- Stay in their home, with modifications and assistance as needed.
- Move into another private residence that better meets their needs.
- Move in with relatives, or invite relatives to move in with them.

Home Sweet Home. Many people want to remain in their homes as they get older. Eldercare experts refer to this choice as "aging in place." In many cases, this will require physical modifications to the home to make it safer and more comfortable for older adults. People who decide to age in place often also need assistance with both personal care and household tasks.

Most homes, especially older houses, are not designed for people with physical limitations or impairments. Helpful modifications often include (but are not limited) to the following:

- Elevated toilet seats and grab bars in the bathrooms
- Ramps
- Wider doorways
- Non-slip materials in bathrooms
- Safer, more accessible tubs and showers
- Brighter lighting, especially in the bathroom and kitchen
- Lever-style door handles

If your parents choose to remain in their home, then they will eventually need outside help—which means a lot of work for you, even if you enlist siblings or hire people to help you with the caregiving jobs. Of course, bringing in paid support for your parents has its own challenges. If you decide to do the hiring yourself, you've got to find the help, oversee the work, and manage the schedules. You can simplify this process by using an in-home care agency, which has a roster of qualified employees available to perform these jobs.

If possible, involve your parents in the hiring process. When Mom and Dad help hire the people who come into their home, they are less likely to complain about or fire them, because they are partially responsible for the hiring decisions.

I learned this the hard way. After months of cleaning my parents' house and mowing their lawn, I hired other people to do these jobs. But when I sent over my own cleaning person, my parents fired her and told me that I did a better job. I found someone to mow the lawn, but they fired him and informed me that he "didn't do it like Barbara." Exasperated, I gritted my teeth and took on the cleaning and the mowing again.

Later on, I had enough perspective to realize two things. One: I should have treated my parents as adults and consulted them during the hiring. Two: My parents had been scared. They were afraid that once I found someone else to do the work, I wouldn't come by to see them anymore. I wish I had known enough to sit down, hold their hands, and tell them, "Having outside help means that I can spend more time with you, instead of rushing around working. I'm not hiring people so I can avoid you. I'm not going to disappear. I am going to be here."

Moving to a *new* Home Sweet Home. *Now* might be a great time for Mom and Dad to downsize. Independent parents may be ready for less square footage, fewer responsibilities, and more companionship. Look for housing that follows the principles of "universal design." These buildings are constructed to be accessible to everyone and will require fewer modifications as your parents get older.

A move into a **condominium** can make life easier by reducing home maintenance chores and simplifying finances. Some seniors opt for **shared housing** and combine resources with friends or siblings or unrelated peers by moving into a single dwelling or a set of apartments. A newer trend, known as **co-housing**, has resulted in the construction of mini-developments designed to create friendly, interdependent senior neighborhoods. **Active adult communities** cater to people over 55 by offering condo and/or apartment living combined with social activities. These communities may have pools, fitness rooms, classes, and other amenities. Members pay homeowner association fees that cover most exterior maintenance costs.

The coming-to-live-with-you question. As soon as you and your parents begin to discuss housing, the possibility of moving in with you will come up. Sharing a home with your parents is a fairly common occurrence. According to the Pew Research Center, the number of American seniors who live alone has been slowly declining. Pew also notes that approximately 20 percent of the over-65 population now lives in a multigenerational household.

Some parents will refuse to move in with their children under any circumstances, but most will assume that living with you is an option. If you do not plan on inviting your parents to live with you, then share this information with your mother and father. Do not be evasive or vague. Be **very clear** in order to prevent misunderstandings and false hopes.

On the other hand, if you plan to suggest that Mom and Dad move in with you, then consult with your spouse and children *before* you say a word about this to your parents. **Do not take this option lightly.** Having Mom and Dad move into your house can appear to be the simplest, least expensive, and most expedient choice, but don't be fooled. Of all the possible housing options, this one requires the most advanced planning, discussion, and cooperation from family members. Talk at length with your spouse and children about the potential effects on their lives. Pay special attention to your spouse's concerns. In a survey conducted by Caring.com, 80 percent of caregivers said that caring for aging parents placed stress on their marriage.

When parents come to live with you, every aspect of your life is affected: your immediate family, your marriage, your personal time and space, your finances, your social network, and your career. For some families, living with three generations under one roof strengthens bonds and enriches daily life; for others, having grandparents in the house turns into a disaster.

The home of an adult child isn't the only possibility for a senior who wants to share living space with family. Sometimes a parent will consider moving in with a sibling or other relative, or may invite a relative or friend to come live with them. These situations are less common, but the same considerations apply.

House rules and exit strategies. Before Mom and Dad are going to move in, have several group discussions with them and your immediate family to determine what everyone expects. Everyone should collaborate to establish house rules about meals, chores, sleeping arrangements, finances, transportation, and other aspects of daily life. Have a frank discussion about how to accommodate everyone's need for privacy.

I recommend welcoming your parents into your home for a *trial period*. Once the trial period is over, your family and your parents can decide whether this is a practical arrangement. If everyone agrees to continue living together, then discuss an "exit strategy." As your parents' health and capabilities diminish over time, living with you may become impractical. Never assume that the initial circumstances will remain the same. Change is inevitable.

The "two-person nursing home." Whether your parents live in their home or your home, caregiving can be a big job. As Mom and/or Dad age in place and need assistance, you become the manager of a tiny, two-person, 24-hour-a-day nursing home. Hiring a "staff" may be essential to maintaining your own physical and mental health. Your parents may also require a level of care that you cannot provide by yourself. As the manager, you can handle all the hiring yourself or you can enlist the aid of an in-home care agency. In that case, the agency would assume responsibility for the vetting, background checks, hiring, and scheduling of workers, which may include nurses, home healthcare aids, companions, and housekeepers.

Aside from preventing burnout, hiring help can also protect your financial health. According to AARP, people over 50 who leave their jobs to caregive often lose hundreds of thousands of dollars in wages, pension benefits, and other income. Actual losses for the average caregiver come to over $300,000.

Your parents may require the services of the following types of assistants:

- **Nurses**. These trained professionals perform skilled healthcare tasks such as administering medicines, drawing blood, injecting insulin, and checking for bruises, bedsores, and other injuries. Nurses can also assess Mom's and Dad's physical, mental, and cognitive health between doctor appointments and alert you to problems. Nurses are considered "skilled" healthcare employees.
- **Home healthcare aides.** Aides help elders with showering, bathing, dressing, and other tasks related to personal care. In the healthcare industry, these types of services are referred to as "unskilled."

- **Personal companions.** Companions can offer support for your parents in a variety of ways, including meal preparation, light housework, socializing, physical exercise, shopping, outings, and overnight supervision.
- **Housekeepers.** Depending on your parents' needs, these workers can handle light or heavy housekeeping, cooking, and other household tasks.
- **Outdoor service people.** As parents get older, it is often helpful or necessary to hire workers to do exterior maintenance tasks, such as gardening, lawn-mowing, and snow-shoveling.

Other useful resources you may wish to seek out include the following:

- **Transportation services.** These include door-to-door van service, buses, taxis, and volunteer drivers.
- **Meal delivery.** This service is available from many restaurants, and most offer carry-out. Meals on Wheels provides over 1 million meals to seniors every day, either through individual deliveries or in group settings such as senior centers.
- **Food delivery.** This service is offered by many grocery stores. A fee or minimum purchase amount is usually required.
- **Other delivery services.** Delivery service is sometimes available from dry cleaners, laundries, libraries, etc.
- **Home visits.** Visits to your parents' home can be arranged with professional services or volunteers.
- **Live or automated check-in calls and reminder services.** These services can provide socialization, updates on your parents' conditions, or reminders for appointments, medications, and other daily tasks.
- **Senior centers.** Senior centers play an important role in many communities and offer a centralized location for many kinds of services and opportunities, including classes, recreation, meals, healthcare services, access to social workers, and advice or assistance with financial matters such as tax preparation and insurance.

- **Adult daycare centers.** These centers offer daily supervised activities, socializing, and meals for seniors. Many centers feature flexible programs, allowing seniors to attend part-time or as needed.
- **Respite care services.** These organizations can give *you* a break from caregiving for any length of time, from a few hours to a few weeks. They can also provide access to information, referrals, and support groups.
- **Hospice.** Hospice can provide invaluable care and support during the last six months of life.
- **The local Agency on Aging**. Your area's Agency on Aging and other, national associations dealing in eldercare issues stand ready with information, referrals, and other helpful services. (For more information, see **Resources** at the back of this book.)

Personalized professional help for *caregivers* is also available to help you deal with the many demands that caregiving places on you. Running a "two-person nursing home" is a demanding, time-consuming job. Consider enlisting the help of a **Geriatric Care Manager (GCM)** to ease the burdens of caregiving—especially if you are a long-distance caregiver.

Employing a GCM is an added expense, but these professionals are talented, fast, capable, and have access to a network of services that can save you time and money in the long run. Your GCM will assess your parents' needs, determine your ability to help them, and then make recommendations on how to move forward. A GCM will provide assistance with complicated issues such as Medicare, insurance, and medical care, as well as step in for you as needed at doctors' appointments. A GCM can also act as a third party to council your parents on issues such as driving and housing. For long-distance caregivers, GCMs also serve as local contacts to help with everyday issues such as hiring in-home care, and provide crisis management during emergencies. The website Caremanager.org is a good place to start looking if you are interested in finding a GCM.

If you are retrofitting your home or your parents' home to improve safety and accessibility, you can hire a **Certified Aging-in-Place Specialist (CAPS)**. This professional knows precisely how to modify a home to create a better, safer, more comfortable environment for your parents. CAPS is a designation created by the National Association of Home Builders.

Option 2: *Living in a Senior Community or Facility*

Time for a change. If you are currently running that "two-person nursing home" and feel overwhelmed, I want to tell you that **it is *okay* to tell your parents, "I love you, but I can't do this anymore."** You may be neglecting your family, your job, or yourself because of all the demands on your time and energy. Your parents might have developed physical problems, dementia, or depression and can no longer live safely in a standard residence. You may also have financial reasons. At some point, the costs of caring for parents at home may outpace the expense of an assisted living or skilled nursing facility.

I labored to keep my parents in their home longer than I should have. I didn't have the energy to convince them to move into a retirement community and then to orchestrate the move. So I hopped from crisis to crisis, solving problems as they came along. I avoided looking very far ahead down the road. I have no idea how long my parents would have stayed in their house if my father hadn't been scammed out of $68,000. Once my mother found out, she was so angry that she saw the move as an opportunity to "get back" at my dad. Since he didn't want to move, she was going to seize this opportunity and make him do it! Looking back, I am almost glad that Dad lost that money, because the crisis gave me a remarkable chance to change my parents' lives in a very positive way.

This crisis also allowed me to see that I was not a failure simply because I could no longer run that personal nursing home for my parents. For years, I clung to the idea that I was a terrible daughter if I didn't make it possible for my parents to live in their house until they died. It's very hard for caregivers, particularly daughters, to admit that they can't take care of their parents any longer. Yet, once I accepted the situation, moving my parents to a continuing care retirement community turned out to be one of the best choices that I—and they—ever made.

The benefits of moving. Moving into a facility designed especially for seniors can have significant benefits for both parents and caregivers. Here are just a few of them:

- **Assistance and medical help are always available.** You can depend on the staff to help your parents, day or night. You won't be interrupted at work by a phone call from Dad complaining that his home healthcare aide didn't show up and now he can't get into the shower. You can go away for a weekend without constantly worrying that Mom will trip over the rug, break her hip, and lie helpless on the floor until you return.

157

- **Finances are simpler**. Moving to a facility cuts down on the number of individual expenses because costs are bundled together. In addition, consistent monthly expenses make budgeting easier.
- **Safety features are designed specifically for seniors**. Ordinary bathrooms and kitchens are dangerous places for older people. Sharp corners, small spaces, and hard, slippery surfaces make these rooms the worst spots for accidents. Senior facilities are carefully designed to maximize safety.
- **Meals are provided**. Nutritious food is served on a schedule, which helps your parents stay healthy and relieves them of the challenges of cooking. Eating meals in the dining room one to three times a day also encourages Mom and Dad to wake up at a regular time, shower, get dressed, and spend time socializing.
- **There are plenty of opportunities for socialization, physical activity, and mental stimulation.** A study by the Harvard School of Public Health found that social interactions can slow age-related decline in memory up to 50 percent. The activities in a senior-focused facility are varied and specifically tailored to residents' interests. My parents' options included exercise classes, lectures, games and cards, sing-alongs, movie nights, studio art and craft classes, lectures, and visits from outside groups such as school choirs and zoos.
- **Visitors are welcome**. Once my parents moved into their own apartment in a continuing care retirement community, the kids loved to visit them. They called Grandma and Grandpa's new home "Camp Hyatt," because of the delicious meals and constant activities and socializing. I also enjoyed my visits more because I could actually sit down and talk with Mom and Dad, instead of cleaning and cooking for them. I could just *be* with them.

The challenges of moving. Finding the right place for your parents is not a simple task. As the caregiver, you will probably shoulder most of the burden of researching and visiting various facilities as well as downsizing and moving your parents. Enlisting the help and advice of other family members in these efforts is essential.

Even after Mom and Dad have moved into their new home, you will still have plenty to do. After my parents moved into an apartment in a continuing care retirement community, I would visit them nearly every day to chat, check on their general health, help with the laundry, and make sure they were participating in activities and eating properly. At the same time, I had been relieved of many other caregiver responsibilities, so these tasks felt less burdensome.

I was fortunate—the first facility that my parents moved into was a great fit, and they stayed there for the rest of their lives because they were able to transition into a higher level of care on the same campus as it was needed. Despite your best efforts, though, the first facility that your parents choose may not turn out to be their best option. Further moves can be precipitated by issues ranging from small ones (such as hating the food) to huge ones (such as the death of a spouse). In addition, your parents' physical or cognitive status may change significantly over time, making their current level of care inadequate. In these cases, you will need to start looking at housing again.

Finding the right place for your parents. When your parents move to a long-term housing facility, they essentially have five possible destinations, each designed for safe, comfortable, and supportive senior living. As a reminder, here they are again:

1. Independent living communities
2. Continuing care retirement communities (CCRC), which offer a range of housing from independent living to skilled nursing
3. Assisted living facilities
4. Skilled nursing facilities
5. Facilities designed specifically for patients with dementia

Selecting the right facility for your parents means reviewing your assessments and helping Mom and Dad find the best fit for their needs. Within each grouping, individual facilities will have their own specialties and amenities

Housing Option 1: *Independent living communities.* Independent living communities offer private apartments and/or condominiums for people over 55 who have few or no medical problems. Most residents can perform the basic acts of daily living by themselves. They don't need help getting dressed, eating, getting in and out of bed, controlling elimination and urination,

159

or conducting tasks involving personal hygiene and grooming. Some residents have mobility issues but can independently maneuver themselves using walkers or wheelchairs. For greater comfort and safety, the apartments may be constructed with universal design features such as wider doorways, showers with seating, handrails, and easy-to-grab door and cabinet handles.

For residents who don't drive, most independent living communities offer regular shuttles to transport residents to stores, entertainment venues, and other locations. Many communities offer fitness centers and pools, as well as social activities, entertainment, and arts, crafts, and hobby classes. Some also offer daily meals in a central location.

Once my parents adjusted to their new apartment in an independent living community, I no longer felt completely overwhelmed. My kids now eagerly asked, "When are we going to visit Grandma and Grandpa?" instead of dreading our trips to my parents' cluttered, funny-smelling house. The facility's dining room served delicious meals, so we could have a family dinner that I didn't need to cook. I had the opportunity to meet and compare experiences with other caregivers. My parents renewed their social lives and rediscovered rewarding hobbies. I remember arriving at the front desk one afternoon to see a poster announcing that my dad was the euchre champion that week.

I hadn't even known that he could play the card game.

Housing Option 2: *Assisted living facilities.* Assisted living facilities are designed for seniors who need help with some acts of daily living. Housing arrangements resemble private apartments, hotel rooms, or dormitories, and may be private or semi-private. Meals, housekeeping, and laundry services are provided. Assisted living offers many planned activities and opportunities for socializing, as well as individual attention from nurses and other healthcare professionals.

If your parents meet the following criteria, they can benefit from assisted living:

- Can no longer live safely on their own
- Need some help with daily living activities, such as bathing, showering, and using the bathroom
- Need help monitoring their medication
- Are not eating properly
- Are not sleeping on a regular schedule

160

- Face minor mobility challenges
- Do NOT require a high level of nursing or medical care
- Still function cognitively and physically at a high level
- Still interact well with people
- Have a generally high quality of life

Staff and nurses are available 24 hours a day to help your parents. When my mother moved into assisted living, I breathed a big sigh of relief. I didn't have to worry incessantly about her meals, laundry, and medications. But I was surprised to find that the biggest benefit to my parents came from the constant opportunities to interact with other residents and staff members. Seniors living by themselves often become isolated and lonely. Interacting with other people helps prevent depression and can slow age-related memory decline.

I'm convinced that moving to an assisted living facility saved my mom's life. While living for several years in an independent living apartment, her health gradually worsened. She was a "brittle" diabetic and, when her sugar levels spiked rapidly, Mom's solution was to pull the emergency cord in her apartment. All the nurses came running, only to discover that my mother had not been checking her blood sugar or taking her medication . . . again.

The staff started suggesting a move to assisted living and I agreed, but Mom had become intensely stubborn and did not want to cooperate. Then she had a transient ischemic attack (TIA stroke) and had to be admitted into the hospital. After her condition improved, the doctor prescribed some physical therapy at a rehabilitation center.

I decided to take advantage of this health crisis to get Mom into assisted living. So I lied, telling her that after she finished her stint at the rehab center, the doctors wanted her transferred into an assisted living situation until she was strong enough to live on her own. After the move, Mom would periodically inquire about returning to her old apartment. As the weeks passed, though, she stopped asking. She had become comfortable where she was, made new friends, and life in assisted living had become her new "normal."

At first, I felt guilty—good girls don't lie, especially to their *mothers*. But this big fib turned out to be best thing I ever did for her. According to Mom's doctors, she lived at least four years longer than expected because of the superior medical care available in assisted living. In the past, she had paid little attention to her diet, her blood sugar levels, and the timing of her injections.

Now, the nurses monitored her blood sugar and made sure she received her medications. Mom ate regular meals and formed a devoted friendship with another resident. The two ladies spent their days together, going to movies, meals, and exercises classes. I was completely charmed by their friendship, and delighted that my mom's physical and emotional health improved dramatically for several years.

I also learned a very important secret of caregiving: **At some point, loving caregivers may need to lie**. If your parents have cognitive or emotional problems that threaten their health or safety, I give you permission to be vague, avoid specific dates, and resist making promises. I call it "therapeutic fibbing." In these cases, *not* telling the complete truth may allow you to solve difficult problems without distressing your parents.

Housing Option 3: *Skilled nursing facilities.* Skilled nursing facilities—also known as **long-term care facilities**—provide round-the-clock skilled-nursing care for patients who either have serious long-lasting medical issues or who require short-term recovery after hospitalization. The ratio of staff to patients increases dramatically between assisted living and skilled nursing. In a skilled nursing facility, your parents are under the supervision of trained professionals who will monitor their medicines, provide treatments, and insert their IVs. Mom and Dad will also receive any needed support with personal care and other aspects of daily living. Plenty of activities and socializing opportunities are available for the more-able residents.

Every skilled nursing facility has different criteria and accepts different kinds of patients. Look for a place that is tailored to your parents' needs. Your parents should transition into a skilled nursing facility when any of the following conditions arises:

- Your parents' doctors or their current facility advise the move.
- Your parents are unable to adequately perform many of the acts of daily living and need consistent help.
- They are living with you or in their own home, but their needs exceed the level of care that in-home care can provide.
- They require such a high level of physical help and/or constant observation that the staff at their assisted living facility struggles to accommodate them.

- Your parents' mental capabilities have deteriorated to the point where they engage in wandering behaviors, have disruptive sleeping patterns, exhibit inappropriate social interactions, or can't recall when they have eaten.
- You, as the caregiver, already know that they need to move, but they are in denial.

Many parents will resist the suggestion to move into a skilled nursing facility. They may become angry, tearful, or anxious, and accuse you sending them off to "a home." In this case, fear and ignorance are your true enemies here—not your parents. Address your parents' concerns by visiting the chosen facility so that you can report back to them. Take photographs to familiarize them with the building and the staff. Ask Mom and Dad what worries them the most, and then interview the staff and explore the facility so you can address your parents' concerns.

Enlisting a third party, such as their doctor, a geriatric care manager, or representative from the facility, can be very helpful. These professionals are accustomed to explaining the reasons for making this move, and their words may carry more weight than yours.

Housing Option 4: *Continuing Care Retirement Communities* **(CCRC).** A CCRC offers all three types of housing—independent living, assisted living, and skilled nursing—on one campus. The skilled nursing facility may include a dementia unit as well.

My parents moved from their home into a CCRC. At first, they stayed together in an apartment in the independent living section of the facility. My mother had more health problems than my father. This happens to many married couples. As they age, one partner will often decline more quickly than the other and have different needs. During her time in the CCRC, my mother needed all three levels of care at various times. Because the facilities shared the same campus, her transitions between the different levels of care went smoothly for both Mom and Dad, since my father could easily visit her at each location.

Housing Option 5: *Facilities designed specifically for patients with dementia.* Some skilled nursing facilities are designed solely for people with Alzheimer's disease and other types of dementia. Other facilities may have a separate, "locked wing" for Alzheimer's patients, which prevents residents with dementia from wandering out of the facility. These separate Alzheimer's facilities ensure that dementia patients are safe and receive the specialized caregiving and medications tailored to their conditions. Note that the terms "Alzheimer's" and "dementia" are often used interchangeably nowadays, and these facilities go by a number of interchangeable names, including "memory unit," "memory care community," "dementia unit," and "Alzheimer's facility."

How Are *You* Feeling?

Moving your parents is nearly as difficult for you as it is for them. Don't be surprised if you feel **overwhelmed, exhausted**, and **fearful**.

When I was in the middle of moving my parents and preparing their house to be sold, I kept thinking, "This is the worst thing ever!" I spent hours every day sorting through their belongings and cleaning their house. I lost 25 pounds, most of it from anxiety. Looking back, I can see that I made a lot of good decisions, but I had no idea whether my plans would prove successful or disastrous at that time. Back then, I felt unsure and worried constantly.

You may also feel **guilty and resentful**. You encouraged your parents to move and now they are struggling to adapt to a new life. You want to be sympathetic, but you've spent a tremendous amount of time and effort to help your parents, and they may not even appreciate your sweat and tears. In fact, they may be angry and critical. Try to remind yourself that most of your parents' emotions spring from a stressful but *temporary* situation.

Fortunately, you also have a right to feel **grateful and relieved.** You are lifting a great burden from your shoulders and, once the move is over, you will have less stress and worry. These positive outcomes can help balance out the negative emotions.

Downsizing and moving my parents was the most difficult and exhausting experience of my life. But I would do it all over again. That move gave my parents a safe, supportive place to live. It also gave me a priceless gift. Those four years that my mom spent in assisted living were the best years of our entire relationship. She and I ate lunch together and played games together. We giggled together! She became more than my mother, more than my father's wife, more than a daughter's responsibility.

My mom became my friend.

Wiping Dishes

By Jim Berg

My father died suddenly of a heart attack. No warning. Poof. A phone call and he was gone: It was unbearable. Like a limb had been ripped from the family tree.

Within weeks of my father's death, my mother seemed to lose all energy and vitality—as though the only thing that had kept her going was taking care of him. Realizing that she couldn't live on her own, we sold the house and moved her to a retirement center that offered some features of assisted living. Not a fun thing to do: Forcing your mom to sell her house and move.

One Saturday visit, I found her sitting wrapped in a blanket at the window. She smiled warmly and I kissed her on the forehead, then sat down in a chair next to her.

"I ran into Clara Schultz in the lobby," I said.

My mom blew air out of her mouth.

"She says you should come down and play cards sometime."

"Gossip, she means. All they do is sit and gossip."

"Well, it would get you out of this room once in a while."

She blew air out of her mouth again.

When I started unpacking some groceries, she stood and moved unsteadily to the table, ignoring the walker.

"Just sit, okay?" I pulled out a chair at the table for her. "And talk to me while I put these things away."

She sat, and I noticed a smattering of red patches on the underside of her arm. "Have you been using that lotion every day?" I asked.

"Most days," she said. "If I think of it."

When I began washing a stack of dishes in the sink, she stood, bracing herself with her hands on the table, and moved to help me.

"Ma, sit."

"Oh hush," she said. "I gotta do something."

She grabbed a wet plate with the towel, wiped it carefully, and stacked it in the cupboard. I smiled to myself, remembering all the evenings I had wiped dishes at my mother's side when I was a kid. Grabbing the dishes with the towel so that my hand didn't touch them. Holding the knives with the sharp edge away from my body, wiping carefully down the length of the blade. And talking all the while about books and school. Talking about Father Ralph's sermons and the Bible. Talking about whatever needed talking about, each night ending with my mother's sly finale. Pumping too much hand lotion onto her palm, so she had an excuse and an opportunity to wrap her hands in mine. I still remember standing close to her in these moments, the scent of almonds from the lotion filling the air, her hands warm from the dish water.

"Bertha Entner came to visit the other day," she said, interrupting my thoughts.

"Old Lady Entner?"

My mother nods, and I smile broadly. Old Lady Entner was a local legend, a husky farm gal with a swinging bosom and thick arms, who cussed and drank with the men. Years back, I saw her drop her husband with one swift blow at the local tavern.

"How is she? Still beating up the old man?"

"She's fine. Strong as an ox . . . but the language she uses. And the stories she tells."

"Like what?"

"Oh." A coy smile crosses my mother's face. "She was telling me how a bull chased her into the pasture when she was just a girl, and she fell and—"

A sudden spasm shook my mother's body. She brought the towel to her mouth and coughed harshly—a scary wet gurgle—and then glanced at me like a guilty child. "It's getting so I can't move around without coughing."

I sat down next to her, rubbing a hand gently along her bumpy spine, and noticed how her hair had thinned, how the skin hung loosely on her frame. The sudden intuition that I might never see her alive swept through my body.

166

"So what happened?" I asked.

"She was running," my mother said, "as fast as she could, with the bull chasing. She could feel him snorting behind her, but most of all she remembers falling and rolling over in the pasture. . . ." She stopped in midsentence, with that coy smile lifting the corners of her mouth, and then finished, ". . . she remembers falling and lying on the ground with 'all his bull stuff' hanging there just above her."

I broke into choking laughter and my mother laughed, too, until another cough shook her body. She coughed and coughed—her skin flushing red from laughing and coughing. I rubbed her back, felt the spastic surges in her body, and bit my lip in an effort not to laugh. Not to cry.

Resources and Bibliography

Many wonderful informational sites exist. The following lists are a sample of what is available on the internet and do not denote any endorsement on the part of the author.

Barbara McVicker's Websites:

Stuck in the Middle

www.ImStuckintheMiddle.com

Shared stories and tips for caregiving for your elderly parents

Barbara McVicker

www.BarbaraMcVicker.com

Information about the author and her services as a speaker and consultant

Other Resources & Websites:

Caring.com

www.Caring.com

All kinds of caregiver information and support

Family Caregiver Alliance

1-800-445-8106

www.Caregiver.org

Education and training for caregivers

American Assn of Retired Persons (AARP)

1-888-687-2277

www.aarp.org

Advocacy and information for people over 50

American Red Cross

1-800-RED-CROSS

http://www.redcross.org/www-files/Documents/pdf/training/FamilyCaregiving.pdf

Caregiving courses

ARCH Respite

www.archrespite.org

Resources for respite care

The Boomer Burden

www.theestatelady.com

Dealing with the accumulation of stuff

Meals on Wheels Association of America
1-703-548-5558
www.mowaa.org
Hot food delivery for the elderly

National Clearinghouse for Long-Term Care
www.longtermcare.gov
Long-term care and what decisions need to be made

National Association of Professional
Geriatric Care Managers
1-520-881-8008
www.caremanager.org
Referral listing

National Alliance for Caregiving
www.caregiving.org
Guides and resources for family caregiving

National Family Caregiving Association
1-800-896-3650
www.nfcacares.org

They're Your Parents, Too!
www.yourparentstoo.com
Effects of caregiving for parents on adult siblings

AGING

Alliance for Aging Research
1-202-293-2856
www.agingresearch.org
Non-profit supporting discoveries to improve aging and health

Administration on Aging
1-800-677-1116
Information for seniors including Eldercare Locator, benefits, and government programs

Children of Aging Parents
1-800-227-7294
www.caps4caregivers.org
Information, referrals, and support

National Association of Area Agencies on Aging
1-202-872-0888
www.n4a.org
Contact information for your local Area Agency on Aging

National Council on Aging
1-202-479-1200
www.ncoa.org
Resources on health, staying independent, and volunteering

National Institute on Aging
1-800-222-2225
www.nia.nih.gov
Information and research about health and aging

PHYSICAL & MENTAL HEALTH

Helpguide
www.helpguide.org
Noncommercial information on mental health and life-long wellness; links to assessment questions.

Medicare
1-800-MEDICARE
www.medicare.gov
Information about Medicare services

National Alliance on Mental Illness
1-800-950-6264
www.nami.org
Information on many different mental illnesses, especially depression

NIH: Senior Health

www.nihseniorhealth.gov

Popular health topics for older adults

National Institute of Mental Health

www.nimh.nih.gov

Answers to a variety of mental health questions

Visiting Nurse Associations of America

1-800-866-8773

www.vnaa.org

Information about in-home nursing

END OF LIFE

Aging with Dignity

1-888-594-7437

www.agingwithdignity.org

Developed "Five Wishes" to assist families in discussing end-of-life issues

Caring Connections

1-800-989-9455

www.caringinfo.org

Dying and end-of-life resources, including advance directives for every state; free downloads of Medical Power of Attorney forms

Funeral Resources

www.funeralresources.com

Everything you need to know about planning a funeral

Growth House

www.growthhouse.org

Information about terminal illness and hospice

Hard Choices for Loving People
www.hardchoices.com/about_hc.html
Most helpful pamphlet on making difficult end-of-life choices

Hospice Foundation of America
1-800-854-3402
www.hospicefoundation.org
Hospice care improves the quality of a patient's last days by offering comfort and dignity

Kind Ethics
www.kindethics.com
Compassionate decision making for patients who can no longer make their own medical and end-of-life decisions

CONSUMER & LEGAL PROTECTION

American Bar Association: Commission on Law and Aging
1-202-662-8690
www.abanet.org/aging
Help with legal issues

National Academy of Elder Law Attorneys
www.naela.com
A professional association of attorneys who are dedicated to improving the quality of legal services provided to seniors and people with special needs

National Reverse Mortgage Lenders Association
www.reversemortgage.org
The latest information on reverse mortgage options

National Senior Citizens Law Center
1-202-289-6976
www.nsclc.org
Advocates for the elderly on issues of income and health

USA.gov
1-800-FED-INFO
1-800-333-4636
www.seniors.gov
Federal and State aging websites offering health, education, laws, & consumer information, with many facts and links

Bibliography

Abramson, Alexis. *The Caregiver's Survival Handbook (Revised): Caring for your Aging Parents Without Losing Yourself.* Perigee Trade, 2011.

Beerman, Susan and Judith Rappaport-Mission. *Eldercare 911: The Caregiver's Complete Handbook for Making Decisions (Revised, Updated and Expanded).* Prometheus Books, 2008.

Carr, Sasha and Sandra Choron. *The Caregiver's Essential Handbook: More than 1,200 Tips to Help You Care for and Comfort the Seniors in Your Life.* McGraw-Hill, 2003.

Delehanty, Hugh and Elinor Ginzler. *Caring for Your Parents: The Complete AARP Guide.* Sterling Publishing, 2008.

Driscoll, Marilee. *The Complete Idiot's Guide to Long-term Care Planning.* Alpha, 2002.

Dunn, Hank. *Hard Choices for Loving People: CPR, Artificial Feeding, Comfort Care and the Patient with a Life-Threatening Illness.* A & A Publishers, Inc. 2001. Available as a free pdf file at www.hardchoices.com

Fulford, D.G. *Designated Daughter: The Bonus Years with Mom.* Hyperion, 2008.

Gross, Jane. *A Bittersweet Season: Caring for Our Aging Parents and Ourselves.* Vintage, 2012.

Gruetzner, Howard, M.Ed. *Alzheimer's: A Caregiver's Guide and Sourcebook (Third Edition).* John Wiley & Sons, Inc., 2001.

Hagan, Paul. *Stages of Senior Care: Your Step-by-Step Guide to Making Best Decisions.* McGraw-Hill, 2009.

Hall, Julie. *The Boomer Burden: Dealing with Your Parents' Lifetime Accumulation of Stuff.* Thomas Nelson, 2008.

Kardasis, Arline. *Mom Always Liked You Best: A Guide for Resolving Family Feuds, Inheritance Battles, & Eldercare Crisis.* Agreement Resources, 2011.

Karpinski, Marion, R.N. *Quick Tips for Caregivers.* Medifecta Healthcare Training, 2000.

Kind, Viki, M.A. *The Caregiver's Path to Compassionate Decision Making: Making Choices for Those Who Can't.* Greenleaf, 2010.

Loverde, Joy. *The Complete Eldercare Planner: Where to Start, Which Questions to Ask, and How to Find Help.* Three Rivers Press, 2009.

Mace, Nancy L. and Peter Rabins, M.D., MPH. *The 36-Hour Day: A Family Guide to Caring for People Who Have Alzheimer Disease, Related Dementias, and Memory Loss (Fifth Edition).* Grand Central Life and Style, 2012.

McLeod, Beth Witrogen, ed. *And Thou Shalt Honor: The Caregiver's Companion.* Rodale Books, 2003.

Morris, Virginia and Robert Butler. *How to Care for Aging Parents.* Workman Publishing, 2004.

Russo, Francine. *They're Your Parents, Too: How Siblings Can Survive Their Parents' Aging Without Driving Each Other Crazy.* Bantam Books, 2010.

Rust, Mike. *Taking Care of Mom and Dad: The Mechanics of Taking Care of Your Parents in Their Time of Need.* Silver Lake Publishing, 2001.

Safer, Jeanne, Ph.D. *Death Benefits: How Losing a Parent Can Change an Adult's Life – For the Better*. Basic Books, 2010.

Satow, Roberta, Ph.D. *Doing the Right Thing: Taking Care of Your Elderly Parents, Even if They Didn't Take Care of You.* Tarcher, 2006.

Somers, Marion, Ph.D. *Elder Care Made Easier: Doctor Marion's 10 Steps to Help You Care for an Aging Loved One.* Addicus Books, 2006.

About the Author

Barbara McVicker—A nationally-known speaker and eldercare expert, Barbara has appeared in *The Wall Street Journal, AARP, USA Today,* and *Business First.* She has been featured on NPR, FOX, CNN, NBC, and public television. Barbara also works with healthcare providers, caregivers, financial planners, attorneys, senior communities, and Fortune 500 companies. Barbara spent ten years caring for her own parents while juggling a family and career. That life-changing experience led her to pursue a career in eldercare.

Barbara hosted and co-produced the public television special, ***Stuck in the Middle: Caring for Mom and Dad***. In this helpful and heartfelt special, Barbara prepares adult caregivers to face the challenges of caring for their parents. Viewers learn how to assess their parents' needs, gather essential documents, communicate with their siblings, and build a successful caregiving team.

Barbara has written two books and a workbook about caregiving:
> *—Stuck in the Middle: Shared Stories and Tips on Caring for Mom and Dad.*
> *—Before Things Fall Apart: Preparing to Care for Mom and Dad.*
> *—Before Things Fall Apart: The Essential Workbook on Caring for Mom and Dad.*

Your business or organization can benefit from Barbara!

SPEAKER—Barbara loves to talk to audiences about caregiving and eldercare. She provides keynotes and workshops to corporations, conferences, and associations. As an educator and storyteller, Barbara is interactive, informative, and entertaining. She speaks on a wide variety of topics related to eldercare and caregiving, and will individually tailor her presentations on request.

CONSULTANT—As an eldercare expert, Barbara works with healthcare professionals, caregivers, financial institutions, and HR wellness teams. She also trains sale personnel. With Barbara's help, businesses and organizations learn how to provide optimum support for employees facing the challenges of caregiving while working.

MEDIA—Barbara is available for TV, radio, and print interviews. She is also available to write articles for publication.

> TO CONTACT BARBARA
> For speaking engagements: www.BarbaraMcVicker.com
> For caregiver support: www.ImStuckintheMiddle.com
> For email: Barbara@BarbaraMcVicker.com
>
> TO ORDER BARBARA'S BOOKS
> Go to Barbara's websites: www.BarbaraMcVicker.com and www.ImStuckintheMiddle.com.
> Also available on Amazon.
>
> To order Karen Taylor-Good's music, go to: www.karentaylorgood.com.